Open Source Leader

Open Source Leader
The Future of Organizations

Sangeeth Varghese

Foreword by
John P. Kotter

PORTFOLIO
PENGUIN

PORTFOLIO
Published by the Penguin Group
Penguin Books India Pvt. Ltd, 11 Community Centre, Panchsheel Park,
New Delhi 110 017, India
Penguin Group (USA) Inc., 375 Hudson Street, New York, New York 10014, USA
Penguin Group (Canada), 90 Eglinton Avenue East, Suite 700, Toronto, Ontario,
M4P 2Y3, Canada (a division of Pearson Penguin Canada Inc.)
Penguin Books Ltd, 80 Strand, London WC2R 0RL, England
Penguin Ireland, 25 St Stephen's Green, Dublin 2, Ireland (a division of Penguin
Books Ltd)
Penguin Group (Australia), 250 Camberwell Road, Camberwell, Victoria 3124,
Australia (a division of Pearson Australia Group Pty Ltd)
Penguin Group (NZ), 67 Apollo Drive, Rosedale, North Shore 0632,
New Zealand (a division of Pearson New Zealand Ltd)
Penguin Group (South Africa) (Pty) Ltd, 24 Sturdee Avenue, Rosebank,
Johannesburg 2196, South Africa

Penguin Books Ltd, Registered Offices: 80 Strand, London WC2R 0RL, England

First published in Portfolio by Penguin Books India 2010

Copyright © Sangeeth Varghese 2010

All rights reserved

10 9 8 7 6 5 4 3 2 1

The views and opinions expressed in this book are the author's own and the facts
are as reported by him which have been verified to the extent possible, and the
publishers are not in any way liable for the same.

ISBN 9780670083268

Typeset in Sabon MT by Eleven Arts, New Delhi
Printed at Gopsons Papers Ltd., Noida

To Annu, as always

Contents

Acknowledgements

This book was initially meant to be just a collection of interviews—of leaders and organizations—who dared to open up authority and power to all their people, rather than keep it close to their own chest. However, my interviewees were kind enough not only to spare several days of their valuable time, but also to let me snoop around in their offices, hangars, coaching camps and ashrams, to let me discover a clear pattern, which I believe is the future of leadership.

My thanks to Prof. John P. Kotter, someone who has always believed in the potential of what we are trying to do, be it through this book or through the larger vision of creating a leadership democracy, where everyone has an equal opportunity to lead, irrespective of their birth and living conditions.

Jehangir Pocha, the previous editor of *Businessworld*, always wanted this to be the first joint publication between *Businessworld* and Penguin Portfolio. Unfortunately, that did not happen. Yet Jehangir believed in the idea behind this book and believed that this could make an impact on the world of leadership.

I would like to thank Prosenjit Dutta, the current editor of *Businessworld*, who published my first book, and who has always played a critical role in sharpening my ideas and theories.

To Anish Bhambal, associate director, LexisNexis, and earlier head of books at *Businessworld*, who believed that this is a critical idea in the world of leadership and was willing to go an extra mile for it, my special thanks.

S. Seethalakshmi, metro editor, the *Times of India*, Bangalore, and Joseph Hoover, sports editor, *Deccan Chronicle*, have been kind enough to connect me to the right people and have been helpful with their wonderful insights.

My special thanks to Frederick Allen, my editor at Forbes.com, who helped me explore ideas and themes, typically unorthodox for a leadership column. Many of those ideas added to the sharpening of this book.

I wish to place on record my thanks to Jayaraj Sundaresan, scholar from the London School of Economics (LSE) and a great friend, whose discussions revealed to me some great insights, helping me tie up some of the loose threads in this book.

Balasubramaniam Meghanathan was always there to help me with some wonderful research on leaders and organizations, whenever I was getting ready for an interview.

My thanks to Mohammad Nibras and Vidyadhar Prabhudesai, research managers at LeadCap Ventures, who helped me with some great inputs—be it in terms of content or even in terms of the current title.

To all LeadCappers across the world who continue to believe in a vision of a true leadership democracy—thank you.

My thanks to Saroja Khanna of Penguin.

Most importantly, my very warm appreciation to my editor, Heather Adams, who not only believed in the potential of this book, but also was kind enough to guide me in every step.

Foreword

Why the current world needs more leaders

Technological advances and globalization are two very powerful forces that are making our world change more and more, faster and faster, and in more dramatic leaps. Even low-tech industries are feeling the effects of technology. For example, retail stores. Their approach is not much different from what it was a century ago—they still receive goods and check people out with those goods. However, the fact is that they are changing—more swiftly—and more than ever—in terms of technology, in terms of globalization. In fact, it is hard to find any organization that is not being bumped in some ways by the new forces of change. In our modern world, a decision can be made in Frankfurt which affects an enterprise in San Jose, California, which then leads to the growth or shrinkage of a business in Hyderabad.

In such a challenging world, we need leaders—more than ever before and more leaders than ever before. A small store or a large nation can suffer greatly without the leadership needed to help it keep up, adapt, or, best yet, move ahead of other organizations. We need more leaders to help governments and businesses handle all the changes in ways that serve customers, employees, owners and society. Hence, we also cannot afford to restrict leadership just to the top-management positions. Every employee, every citizen should rise to a leadership role. They should step in to solve customer problems; they should step in to solve internal company problems; they should step in to solve society's problems.

Shortcomings of rigid hierarchies

However, enterprises that are currently run solely by strong, rigid hierarchies with a leader at the top have many shortcomings—the primary one being the feeling of infallibility on the part of the leaders. With such a feeling, a leader never finds the sense of urgency needed in a fast-moving world. Organizations find instead a complacency that increasingly becomes their death sentence. Even if leaders are larger than life, they will never be able to see all the new threats and opportunities. Even if the leader could see all that is happening, there is insufficient time to tell people what to do. And even if the leader really is exceptional, when he or she retires, there is an inevitable vacuum at the top which can lead to very unpleasant outcomes.

Such organizations cannot pass on and process relevant information fast enough any more. They can easily waste the brains at the bottom of the pyramid—often in the middle too—in a world that needs more and more brains to find new ideas and innovate. They can demotivate well-educated employees unless they are at the top—at a time when you need motivated people to provide sufficient energy to deal with technological change and globalization.

Ironically, many organizations and people think that this is the only way, primarily because they are anchored in their traditions—a very powerful force. If we were raised to think one way, shifting of beliefs to deal with new realities does not come easily. As we are raised in the midst of a hierarchy-led culture, we often do not try what we know is actually needed, because we do not have faith that we can make a difference. We are not sure whether that change will stick, whether it will be successful or not.

What helps organizations to open up their leadership?

Not all organizations are stuck. In the US, a growing number of enterprises are trying, with some success, to encourage more people at more levels to provide the leadership needed in their jobs. General Electric (GE) has been the classic case for decades. Today, some high-tech companies are being forced, just to keep up, to focus on leadership development. But even with effort, places like Google struggle to produce nearly the number of leaders they need.

Competition often encourages this trend by putting pressure, where a lack of sharing produces poorer and poorer results. So does a visionary leader at the top who recognizes that he or she cannot do the job alone. Such leaders encourage power sharing because they realize that sharing power does not create problems, especially a loss of sufficient control to do a job. They expect more people, at more levels, to provide the leadership needed in their jobs to help the corporation excel. Hence, more people would accept responsibility to develop their own leadership potential and the potential of their subordinates. More people than ever before would be willing to stand up and lead.

How can we find and nurture more leaders?

Finding potential leaders is easier than most people think. There are many individuals with at least a bit of leadership potential. Formal education can help in nurturing this, but nothing substitutes for personal experience—having the room to lead on the job. Leaders need to expect, help, and reward people who grow. Leaders need to convince their people that the glass ceiling has been taken away and that they want their people to grow. Deeds are more important than words. When you demonstrate what you say about who is promoted, how far they are promoted, and what development opportunities are really available, people will self-monitor. They will automatically ask: Does my (different) approach, priorities and agendas help us move towards the bigger vision?

This book will make you think of what possibilities can exist if more opportunities are opened up to develop the leadership potential of more people in our organizations. It will make you think about what will happen if you truly empower all the people below you in your workplace. It will help you think about life, and how it feels living in the twenty-first century, yet in communities that feel like the past. This book will help you think about the future.

June 2010   John P. Kotter

John P. Kotter, Konosuke Matsushita Professor of leadership, Emeritus, at Harvard Business School, is widely regarded as the world's foremost authority on leadership and change. His is the premier voice on how the best organizations actually 'do' change.

He has published seventeen books, twelve of which have been business best-sellers and six of which have won awards or honours. With millions of copies sold, his books have been translated into dozens of languages. His international best-seller Leading Change—*which outlined an actionable, eight-step process for implementing successful transformations—became the change bible for managers around the world.*

Introduction

Why Open Source Leadership Is the Inevitable Future of Organizations

1

In this section:
- Where is our world of leadership heading?
- Why organizations refuse to evolve even as the rest of the world is doing so
- Why the time has come for organizations to evolve into open formats
- Why adopting open leadership formats is mission-critical for organizations
- How open leadership formats provide an evolutionary edge
- Open Source leadership: The open but secret code

Where is our world of leadership heading?

Leadership is changing. In almost every cross section of society, though it started in closed formats—with power and authority concentrated on one or a few selected persons—it is flowing down to the rest of the members by actively embracing open formats, just as water flows from a higher plane towards a lower one. For example, though nation states started out with autocratic rulers who amassed wealth all to themselves, power eventually reached the masses through democracy. Or the family system, though initially monopolized by men through closed patriarchal settings, evolved towards the modern-day egalitarian one.

Social structures like nation states and families evolved from closed formats towards open formats. Leadership, as well as the decision making associated with it, grew into a state where it was

1

no longer monopolized by an individual, but distributed across its members, guaranteeing everyone a certain amount of rights, power and voice—all this while preserving the core of what these social structures are about.

However, most corporate organizations—again an integral part of our social structure, just like nation states and families—are still stuck in their closed formats. As Noam Chomsky, the American linguist and philosopher, puts it, 'A corporation is about the closest thing to a totalitarian institution that humans have ever contrived. There is a convergence of total power at the top. All the decision making lies with either the CEO or the board of directors or both, while orders are transmitted down to the lower levels, from where complete subservience is expected. The people at the top not only assert themselves, but also constantly forbid and suppress any criticism and opposition that might be directed against their agenda.'

Most corporate leaders, even the most celebrated ones, unfortunately are still stuck with the closed format of leadership. Albert Dunlap, the former CEO of Scott Paper and then Sunbeam, who called himself 'Rambo in Pinstripes', is a typical example. He was much written about because he could turn around troubled companies like a charm. However, he also did this by concentrating the entire power upon him. He treated everyone else in the company as if they were disposable inanimate things, not capable of doing anything of their own, unless dictated from the top. He indulged in relentless employee firings and numerous plant closings. He was convinced, as much as many around him, that nothing could be done without him.

Jack Welch, who adorned America's loftiest executive perch close to two decades, is another appropriate example to understand the point of closed leadership perpetuating in our organizations. Welch's resolution was about driving up the productivity in GE, by whatever means. He shut down factories, reduced payrolls and cut lacklustre old-line units, all the while pushing his theory that only shareholders and nothing else mattered. Jack Welch was eventually crowned the 'Manager of the Century', and was celebrated across media, not because he built an open institution—ironically in a country that vouched by open values—but because he managed to build up a behemoth, where closed values were unashamedly practised and individual voices where blatantly squashed.

However, it is natural for us to feel that these are offbeat organizational cases, blown out of proportion. We decided to ask a sample of employees, 500 of them, working in 190 large and medium private corporations in three countries—the USA, the UK and India. Our respondents were randomly drawn from across levels—lower, middle and senior (other than CEOs and board members, of course)—and across industries. Results of this study, done through a short questionnaire, which guaranteed absolute confidentiality to the participants, reiterated our hypothesis. Under 4 per cent of the total sample, that too all of them belonging to the senior management cadre, claimed that they ever felt truly empowered to take decisions. Interestingly, one-fifth of our respondents, at some point of time in their current company, tried to take their own decisions, but felt cheated, as they were not given full organizational support. Almost all of them felt that despite all the talks about open values and freedom in their organizations, their role was actually limited to carrying out the orders given by their seniors. None, absolutely none of these employees, irrespective of their levels, industries or nations that they came from, responded that they had absolute clarity about the paths they took in their organizations.

Vijaya Menon, head of marketing (while this book was being written), at Kingfisher Red, a low-cost airline in India, worked under Vijay Mallya. Mallya, known to be the glamour king of the Indian corporate sector, has splurged money on an F1 and an Indian Premier League Cricket team. However, glamour ends right there, in his external pomp and glory, according to Vijaya. 'Mallya has managed to build a highly competitive and professional team, yet it is almost a dictatorial regime. In internal company meetings, when he is present, we have trained ourselves to meekly sit back and listen. He talks and no one else. Not even questions or doubts.' Vijaya specifically remembers a meeting where a new concept of Kingfisher Airlines was being presented—a meeting attended by all the company's high officials, including the executive vice-president from the company, supposedly in charge of everything. 'I expected this meeting to be different, but unfortunately there were no surprises. No one spoke except Mallya. He had this air about him that when I know everything, why should anyone else talk?' laments Vijaya.

Sandeep Bhargava is the CEO of Studio18, a large Bollywood studio house in India. Sandeep says that his career is ridden with examples of companies that claim to be professionally managed, but in reality control every aspect of decision making, even the less significant ones. Authority is firmly placed on the shoulders of one leader, who guards it. Sandeep challenges us to randomly pick any media house in India, irrespective of whether they are television companies, advertising agencies, production houses or entertainment companies. They all exhibit the same pattern— where they are very personality- or one-leader driven. So, there is always a Subhash Ghai, a leading Bollywood movie director or a Subroto Roy, owner of a media house or an A.G. Krishnamurthy, chairman of an advertising agency, who not only are the towering personalities behind their businesses, but also are the central points where the smallest of small decisions are being taken. 'In these companies,' says Sandeep, 'designations, be it general manager or director, tend to be just a designation, since all the decisions are made at a central point.'

Ram Mynampatti, a whole-time director and briefly the interim CEO of the now defamed Satyam Computers, sums up the argument about most modern-day organizations being closed very well. In a recent interview given to a newspaper he said, 'Things were deliberately made and so structured that no single leader in Satyam would ever get a complete picture of the company's performance at the operational level. Each of us would be privy to a small slice of the business, regardless of the size.'

Why organizations refuse to evolve even as the rest of the world is doing so

How do we explain the sustenance of closed leadership in corporations, even as other similar building blocks of society have evolved into forms that are more open in their leadership style? Why do some of the most intelligent and well-read people of the world support the concentration of leadership and power among a few individuals, while the potential of the greater masses are suppressed?

We came across two reasons:

Books and thinkers on organizational psychology, management and particularly self-help literature have had a large role to play in this. They somehow picked up and celebrated a belief that the people at the top of any organization have a disproportionate influence on its success. The Father of Management, Frederick W. Taylor, is definitely one such person to be blamed, who more than a century ago, helped firmly establish a rigid hierarchy with his theory of 'brains at the top, hands at the bottom'—popularized through his writings. Under Taylorism, actual thinking or initiative on the part of 'the hands' was actively discouraged, as it would potentially undermine the leadership of 'the brains'.

> Reason one for organizations refusing to evolve: Popular magazines and media continue reiterating the Taylorian myth of 'brains at the top, hands at the bottom' in organizations.

Dr John Maxwell, celebrated leadership author, who strives towards building more leaders across the world, has yet another theory for why organizations are not yet evolving. He suggests that different institutions and different communities need not evolve at the same pace. 'When a transition happens, it does not simultaneously happen in all groups. A few groups will emerge as front-runners. When that transition is successful, it starts spreading to the other groups.'

'Corporate organizations have been slow mainly because money is involved. Whenever money is involved, power is involved. People who have the money are least likely to want to open that up and share that. In businesses, one who has the golden goose sets golden rules. But eventually, the power equations here again will change. For sure,' concludes Dr Maxwell.

> Reason two for organizations refusing to evolve: Organizations unfortunately have been laggards in their evolution towards open formats.

Why the time has come for organizations to evolve into open formats

Alex Haslam, professor of social and organizational psychology at the University of Exeter, suggests that though management books initially harped on a 'great man idea' (about a great man qualified to lead, by virtue of some special qualities which set him apart from the other people), several problems showed up when academics and theoreticians started studying these distinguishing attributes. None of them could come up with any convincing answers about any extraordinary powers which these leaders possessed compared to others.

They increasingly came to the conclusion that the people they studied were not great leaders because of any special qualities, but because of the greatness of the groups that they led. Leadership effectively became not an individual trait, but a group trait. 'And this shift in perspective forced the world to see leadership not as a process that revolved around individuals acting and thinking in isolation, but as a group process in which a leader and his people are joined together in a shared endeavour,' says Alex Haslam.

Reason one why this is the right time for organizational transformation to open leadership formats: In academic circles and popular literature, the 'great man idea' of leadership is giving way to group leadership.

Dr John Maxwell thinks that this shift of focus from one great man to the shared efforts in academics, popular literature and media, would hasten the change of closed organizational environments into more open ones. 'In America in the 1980s, if you went to the book store, and if you wanted a business book, you would have picked up a management book, which delved into how to manage people in an organizational context. In the nineties that started changing. The management books started going off the shelf. And they started being replaced with leadership books. The pace of life started to move very fast.

'Until then, the assumption was that everything stays the same. However, as the environment around started moving at a fast pace, people had to catch up with it. That meant they had to lead. The nineties was almost the edge of the leadership book movement. Therefore, leadership became a major subject of learning throughout the world. However, when we came in to this decade we saw another transition—where the focus shifted from one-man-centric leadership books to a team of leaders taking charge. It is no longer one person in charge, but a group of people in charge.

'That was a natural transition, because culture today is a changed one. Things have become so complicated that one person is not able to lead alone. People are also now less willing to take any one person's direction. They want to be equally involved in decision making. They expect dialogues and feedback. Organizational change is faster now than ever before.'

Reason two why this is the right time for organizational transformation to open leadership formats: Fast changing environment is forcing people to look beyond one leader for solutions.

Dr Maxwell says that this increasing complication in the environment has also brought about a self-realization in leaders that they no longer have answers to all the questions.

'In so many years of my interaction with organizations, I am yet to come across a leader who has the capability to lead in every situation, every time and in every area. Leaders who realize this sufficiently early search for others within their organizations who can complete and complement them. Complement them in such a way that they can put their heads together to generate more ideas which in turn could help them compete better in today's competitive marketplace. So, in today's changing world, leaders should understand not only their strengths, but also their weaknesses. Therefore, leaders lead and leaders also follow. Followers follow and they also lead sometimes,' comments Dr Maxwell.

Dr Ram Raghavan, a UK-based consultant who has been studying the human brain for the last couple of decades to develop models to profile people, performance and processes in organizations, reiterates the importance of looking beyond one leader in an organization for all the answers. He has a unique reasoning about this. He says, since the human brain operates at a miniscule 100 hertz (compared to the gigahertz or terra hertz supercomputers of today), it has to screen and process information in the smartest way possible. Hence, although there are designated areas in the brain for certain functions, it also has to draw from and link multiple areas while performing complex tasks. So, even when identical twins experience a specific event, the neural currents generate different imprints and different patterns—enabling different people to have different interpretations of the same event, or enabling them to notice different nuances of the same event. When handling a complicated situation, two brains are always better than one. And five are definitely better than just two.

'It is rather simple. As my friend, Ken Blanchard says, "One of us is not as smart as all of us." Organizational leaders who follow this have made themselves ready for today's marketplace. Else, they would be soon in for a surprise,' suggests Dr Maxwell.

> Reason three why this is the right time for organizational transformation to open leadership formats: Leaders are increasingly becoming self-aware that they are not equipped to do everything alone.

Why adopting open leadership formats is mission-critical for organizations

Beyond the changed realities of today and the self-realization that is dawning upon modern-day leaders, 'social evolution'—where every cross section of society continuously evolves to survive the transformational changes around—is another powerful reason why more organizations would embrace open leadership formats in the future. Social evolution would ensure that organizations not only should be and could be open, but they also would be—whether some of them like it or not. For example, nation states and families advanced towards open formats not because it was politically correct, but because it was made inevitable by their environmental pressures. In short, open formats arrived because it offered evolutionary stability, in the ever-changing scheme of things. Open formats ensured that the competing forces in these social structures became balanced in such a way that they no longer needed to change drastically to fight the constant transformations in the external and internal environments.

The crumbling down of many of the existing traditional closed regimes that we are witnessing, across realms, is not accidental. Anything that did not have the evolutionary stability just had to give in and perish. Hence, eventually every social structure tends to move away from closed formats—characterized by class struggles, conflicts of interests and inequalities—towards open ones, marked by better balance of power and optimization of rewards for groups. Overall, in open leadership formats, social structures enter into a well-oiled machinery mode—almost future ready, which is the reason why organizations should also get there soon.

Organizations would evolve towards open leadership formats because it is the only evolutionary stable form.

How open leadership formats provide an evolutionary edge

Christian List of the London School of Economics and Larissa Conradt of the University of Sussex, in England, who study group decision making in humans and animals, offer us substantial evidence to the fact that the open format is evolutionarily more stable for groups compared to the other forms. One of the important points of evidence that they bring to the table is the cost involved in making decisions in a group. They write that quite contrary to our conventional thinking, under most conditions, the costs to the subordinate group members and to the group as a whole are considerably higher in single-leader closed formats than for open groups.

'Every individual knowingly or unknowingly incurs a cost as a decision is made in a group that he is a part of. This cost to individual group members depends on their own ability to influence the outcome versus that of other group members. For example, when a CEO dictates a corporate decision, it will incur only minimum cost to him because he would choose a decision outcome that is optimal for himself or for his shareholders. However, the subordinate members will incur higher costs according to how different their own optima are from that of the CEO. By contrast, if the group could agree on a decision outcome that is preferred by a majority of members, then the costs would be relatively lower for most members in the group. While the leader alone benefits and pays lower costs in an autocratic group, all other members benefit from an open decision,' write List and Conradt.

Interestingly, the CEO also would incur a cost, even though

he is driving those decisions that are optimal for himself. As subordinates agree to fall in line with his decisions, they are in fact reducing their individual influence, and are giving up on their individual choices and preferences—something which people usually do not want to do. That means a cost to the CEO—the cost of enforcing a decision, typically done in our organizations through means like coercion, manipulation or incentivization. So, open format is not only beneficial for most members in terms of lower costs, but also for the CEO, making it a better long-term proposition compared to closed leadership formats.

> Reason one for the evolutionary advantage of open leadership format: Open leadership considerably lowers the cost for majority of individual members in the organization.

The evolutionary advantage of the open leadership model does not end with lower individual costs. Traditional organizational decisions, even when the leader happens to be the most experienced group member, would incline towards one extreme, since they are taken by one or a few individuals, representing only their vested interests. This extremity in decision making can lead to disasters easily, since a single person would never be able to consider all possibilities and probabilities. In open leadership decision making, every individual has a stake, and hence would be able to add his perspective to it, making the ultimate decision less extreme and hence more realistic.

According to the US political scientist Samuel Huntington, open decision making also helps in better predictability of events, since it engages public expectations, opinions and their preferences within a framework of checks and balances. Without such checks and balances, shocks to the system would have a greater and wider impact. Open leadership formats, which regulate one-man-centric closed decisions, help the overall system to be more resilient and adaptable to the complex and varying environment of today.

Reason two for the evolutionary advantage of open leadership format: Group decisions tend to be less extreme and hence bring in more predictability of results.

Open leadership also has an overall impact on the morale of group members. In a traditional closed leadership set-up, since decisions are imposed on them, people would seldom invest their full potential in carrying them out. Eventually, the group as a whole would lose out, as their performance would be less than optimal at all times. In the longer term, this could mean lower group morale, reduced innovative spirits and lowered competitive advantage.

Dr Ram Raghavan narrates an example drawn from the military, where generals, who are essentially like the CEOs, devise strategies and communicate it downwards for their conversion into tactics and results. Subordinates obey their general and follow orders to implement the strategy devised. Yet, many strategies fail at the ground level because often, subordinates are not truly convinced about the suitability of the strategy, and sometimes do not even believe in the end objectives. As subordinates, they accept the orders and implement them, but as real people, they are not convinced, which leads to failure. Soldiers who have little or no trust in their superiors do not fight to 'win', they fight to 'survive' for another day. Lasting success can only be ensured when generals as well as subordinates are thinking alike.

Reason three for the evolutionary advantage of open leadership format: Open leadership increases stakes of individual members in the system and hence has a positive effect on their overall morale and ultimate results.

Open Source leadership: The open but secret code

Organizations, though currently lagging behind in social evolution, would ultimately take the same route. They would eventually move towards the evolutionary equilibrium offered by open leadership formats.

However, there are a few organizations which stand apart in a crowd of traditional closed ones. They have already taken a step towards being open. This book is about such a state, where some organizations have been forward-looking, to be examples for other traditional closed organizations of today. We refer to this phenomenon as 'Open Source Leadership'. There are two reasons why we have decided upon this name. The first and an obvious one is that many such organizations tend to be from the Open Source software initiatives. However, this concept is not just about Open Source software initiatives and includes several others. So, a second reason for this name revolves around the origin of the term 'Open Source' itself.

Source code is the original version of a software, generally its most versatile, informative and permanent form, allowing the software programmer to communicate with the computer using a reserved set of instructions. It is critical because it serves as a communication tool between the programmers and gives them greater control to tailor- make it to particular requirements. Source code is also a valuable tool for beginners, because without it, they would not be able to study the existing code to gain insights into its techniques.

Many companies and programmers prefer to keep the source code of their software a secret. In fact, they take great pains to keep it close to them, because revealing it would enable others to copy and use it in other programmes. It could even let them search out their vulnerabilities. However, the Open Source software initiative works on the reverse logic. It opens up their most valuable and vulnerable resource—the source code—for scrutiny as well as use, for pretty much everyone who would be interested. Advocates of Open Source point out that this approach makes it possible for a much larger and more diverse set of qualified people to examine their source code, thus providing more and better suggestions for improvements and extensions. Opening up the source also helps a variety of programmers to work together in myriad platforms, thereby popularizing the software much more than if it were to remain a closed one.

After observing the philosophy as well as the success of the some of the Open Source software firms, Henrik Ingo, a software professional and author of the book, *Open Life*, wrote, 'In the world of software, the Open Source movement has successfully challenged traditional ways of thinking. But the software business is only a small part of the world and I believe that other areas of business have a lot to learn from this movement. We all have something to learn from how these people are challenging the traditional mean-spirited business practices without compromising success.'

Open Source leadership would make Henrik Ingo proud. These organizations have already picked up some of the lessons from the Open software world. However, for them, the source code is not a string of programming instructions, but the access to power, authority and influence, which drive their day-to-day operations as well as long-term vision. Traditional organizations, like closed source code software organizations, keep their secret code of power to themselves, while Open Source leadership opens it up. This book focuses on these practices, by delving into the success stories of a few organizations, to demonstrate the point that this is not a utopian dream, but a very practical one, preparing these organizations for a brighter future compared to their traditional closed compatriots.

These organizations are not drawn from any single genre, but from multiple industries and realms. Wikipedia and Linux belong to the Open Source software environment, while Zappos, BCG Consulting, Air Deccan, Biocon, Network18, etc., are private sector corporations. World Cup-winning Hockeyroos and cricket runners-up, the Indian national team, help us learn from the intensely competitive sports world, while Art of Living is from the non-profit sector. The Indian Institute of Science (IISc) is a representative of the educational sector and Narayana Hrudayalaya, of the health care and services sector.

These organizational stories are complemented with several conversations with leadership and organizational experts, like Noam Chomsky, John Maxwell and Alex Haslam.

Our learning about this new concept of Open Source leadership would never be complete, if we were to single-mindedly look at any one of these organizations as such. There are three reasons for this. First, none of these organizations is alike and none of them could be called the flagship. They are all different in their own way, a reflection of the different industries they belong to, innumerable challenges that they face on a daily basis or even the variety of ways in which they have evolved. Second, none of these organizations is complete in their evolutionary process. They are all still progressing from their traditional formats, learning their baby steps towards true openness, at different levels and stages. For example, ICICI Bank, one of the organizations that this book covers, is really in a very rudimentary stage of Open Source leadership, probably even letting us mistake them for a traditional closed one. Yet, what sets them apart is their focus on one of the Open Source leadership attributes—the absence of glass ceilings. They were one of the first organizations, which built strong practices to let women and other minorities compete effectively, demonstrate capabilities and succeed, devoid of any typical invisible corporate barriers. IISc, another example, is at a much more advanced level of Open Source leadership comparatively, where their leadership structures offer equal freedoms to everyone and protect them from the tyranny of the ruling authority. And third, though some of the organizations do not look like Open Source leadership from the outside, they are surprisingly so, as we scratch the surface. For example, the Indian cricket team between 2000 and 2005. It is easy to mistake the team under Sourav Ganguly as a closed and autocratic one. However, it is not so. They are one of the finest examples, and incidentally one of the most successful in their chosen realm. We in fact have some great secrets and stories from the Indian national team dressing room.

In this book, we have woven together eight defining attributes that we most commonly observed in Open Source leadership organizations. These eight attributes are synthesized and crystallized mainly from our conversations with people at all levels in these organizations—juniors, seniors, receptionists, executives, managers, general managers and CEOs. Most conversations were great, and gave us the inputs required for an objective analysis, but at least some of them had a problem, where we thought people were telling us things that we would like to hear. Hence, we complemented these conversations with observations, up close and from far. Observations, especially longer ones, where we almost faded in to the background, separated claims from the truth. We also comprehensively toothcombed secondary sources: academic literature, books, articles, blogs and social networking sites, for further confirmations.

We did not stop at these researches. In fact, we decided to walk our talk. Based on the inspiring learning from the several Open Source leadership organizations that we studied, we overhauled the organization that we run—LeadCap Ventures—the company from where our bread and butter comes. In short, we put our mouth where the money is. The results until now have been encouraging to the point that the concept managed to turn around our sinking company.

Open Source leadership is not a utopian dream. It is not just a 'right thing to do'. It is the evolutionary next phase. Moreover, it is practical. All the lessons contained in this book stem directly from the practical experiences of successful organizations. Hence, we have not limited ourselves with just the definitions of the Open Source leadership attributes, but have delved deeply into specific methodologies that could help other organizations. We hope you find this not just as a nice read, but as a guidebook to evolve and a tool kit to embrace the future.

2

Pink Slip to the CEO
Open Source Leadership Shifts Power from the CEO towards the People

In this section:
- From zero-sum to non-zero sum: Three models towards Open Source leadership
- Why leadership is not about the leader
- How Open Source Leaders are bribing their people to be leaders
- How the Open Source leadership model is eliminating the traditional role of a leader

From zero-sum to non-zero sum: Three models towards Open Source leadership

Linus Torvalds, best known for having initiated the development of the Linux Kernel, once wrote about an interesting transformation: how the practice of alchemy—the medieval forerunner of chemistry but with deep shades of witchcraft—gave way to modern science. Alchemy revolved around a set of secrets, closely guarded by those involved. They made sure that no one came close to their secrets or understood it because their professional success and even existence depended upon these. However, science took exactly the opposite route. It was built on the notion of sharing thoughts, openly developing ideas and improving on other people's initiatives. Unlike alchemy, no single person, even if he was an absolute expert, could monopolize the authority in science. While this openness ensured the success of science and made it what it is today, the secretive path of

17

alchemy led to its failure. It just fizzled out after some time with no trace.

Our traditional closed formal business leaders resemble alchemists more than scientists. The secret leadership ingredient that they guard with their life is their 'power', their ability to exert control over their subordinates. Nici Nelson and Susan Wright, in their book, *Power and Participatory Development*, study how this power affects different actors in an organization using two interesting models—'Power over' and 'Power to'.

'Power over', the first model, considers power as a finite commodity in a closed system, where any party can gain more only at the expense of the other. In short, power is a zero-sum game. The second model, 'Power to', takes a different approach. According to it, power can grow infinitely, if people want it to, just like human potential. Here, power is not a force one exerts in order to prevail or establish barriers over the other, but a motivational force, which is developed in a shared and collective manner.

The first step towards Open Source leadership for traditional organizations is their movement from 'Power over' towards 'Power to'—from a closed zero-sum game, where leaders hoard power all to themselves, towards a shared non-zero-sum game, where leaders consciously reduce their authority. They do this by taking one or more of three routes—a self-enlightened one, a self-interest-driven one or an institution-building one.

Self-enlightened route to Open Source leadership

In a recent article, Michael Lee Stallard, the co-founder of a leadership consulting firm, spoke about the remarkable case of U2. The rock band U2 formed in Dublin, Ireland, have had a phenomenal run since they came together in 1976. Having sold more than 145 million albums worldwide and having won an astonishing twenty-two Grammy awards, they are bigger than almost any other band in history. However, the most interesting aspect about them is the fact that the band members have been together for more than thirty years, a long period, considering that most bands fall apart in less than a decade.

Why has U2 thrived for so long, in an industry where cut-throat competition and backbiting prevail not only among rival groups, but also between band members? Stallard attributes it to a great participatory, consensus-oriented and open culture that U2 promotes inside the band.

U2 is comprised of four band members: lead singer Bono, lead guitar player Edge, bass guitar player Adam Clayton, and drummer Larry Mullen Jr. Among them, Bono is definitely the superstar, where his popularity surpasses that of even most of the Hollywood stars. He was a nominee for the Nobel Peace Prize in 2003, 2005 and 2006 for his philanthropy, and was one of *Time* magazine's '100 Most Influential People' in 2004 as well as 2006, while in 2005 he was the 'Person of the Year'.

Given Bono's status as a megastar, it would not be inconceivable if he claimed more than an equal share of the band's profits or influence. Yet, surprisingly, the economic profits from U2's work are split equally between the four band members and their long-time manager Paul McGuiness. Even in terms of influence over decisions in the band, all the members share an equal portion. The members argue relentlessly over their music and they decide only when all of them agree. Bono does find it frustrating at times, nevertheless U2 follows it as a necessary practice to keep up their culture.

Stallard writes that the band members of U2 have grown to appreciate each other's strengths. Bono once clarified this by pointing towards one of his own weaknesses— although he hears melodies in his head, he is unable to transfer them into written music. Bono considers himself a 'lousy guitar player and an even lousier piano player'. Hence, he has to rely on his fellow band members and recognizes that they are integral to his success. Bono describes U2 as a tight-knit family and community, where each of them shares a commitment to support one another.

In U2, no one has a monopoly. As the most important member and a towering influence, Bono could and should have been the leader according to conventional thinking. However, he has consciously decided to limit his powers so that everyone can share the authority along with him. As Bono once said, 'The way the band functions is even more extraordinary than the band's music.'

Jimmy Wales or Jimbo, as he is popularly known, is an American Internet entrepreneur, and a co-founder and promoter of Wikipedia, a revolutionary open-content encyclopaedia aiming to provide free encyclopaedic information to its readers. 'Imagine a world in which every single person on the planet is given free access to the sum of all human knowledge. That is what we are doing,' Wales outlined his vision for Wikipedia in a 2004 interview with Slashdot. Currently, Wikipedia has over three million articles and close to 2,000 new ones are added on daily, making it the largest encyclopaedia ever assembled, eclipsing even the Yongle Encyclopaedia (1407), which had held its record for nearly 600 years. The surprising element in this is that Wales is not supported by thousands, if not ten thousands of employees to manage this complex affair, but just a small band of voluntary editors, who create a robust, self-regulating community.

However, Wales anticipated nothing more than rubbish, as he started out with his idea of an openly edited encyclopaedia, driven just by volunteers and not paid employees. He says that he used to be so worried during the initial days that he would wake up in the middle of the night, wanting to check the site for vandalism. 'Yet, I resisted the temptation to take over and run it according to my whims and fancies,' he comments. 'Wikipedia evolved as an open system not just through the evolution of time. It is also a natural outcome of who I am—someone who believes in an open structure and in his people.

'I never liked being bossed around myself, and so I am not good at bossing other people around. This might have simply been a reaction against some of my early jobs when I was a teenager—observing authoritarian bosses telling employees what to do, which often led to bad results. Rather, I am a believer in human intelligence—a good leader is not someone who turns his employees into robots suppressing their intelligence, but someone who empowers people to be creative. I prefer a leadership style which is about getting people with the same ideas together and then moving things forward, in a synchronized manner.

'Editors have traditionally wanted top-down control over every detail, but I saw this as counter-productive from the start,' Wales continues. 'In fact, one of the core values that I propagate in Wikipedia is'"Assume Good Faith". If one of us sees someone doing something incorrect in Wikipedia, we should remind ourselves that this person might not be intentionally malicious. He might not have the correct information, or he might not know what we are trying to accomplish. Hence, the first assumption should not be bad about the person, but that he is trying to be helpful.

'This belief has helped me as well as Wikipedia immensely, while creating, editing, managing our vision. And indeed it turns out that most people are trying to do something useful, not something malicious. If we trust people, they do reciprocate in good ways,' says Wales.

Leaders like Bono and Jimmy Wales have chosen the self-enlightened route to move from 'Power over' to 'Power to' to establish Open Source leadership. Both of them realize that a distribution of the power that they hold is required—not because of any external pressures or even self-interest—but because they believe it is the right thing to do. This approach is best captured in Jimmy Wales comment: 'This is the way I am. I am just being myself.' Even as conventional wisdom tells them to hold on to their power, or as they go through instances where things might go wrong, they still resist the temptation to reverse their decision. They continue their movement towards 'Power to'.

> First route towards a non-zero-sum leadership game: Self-enlightened route, where a leader moves away from the closed leadership format not out of any compulsion but out of his own will.

Self-interest-driven route to Open Source leadership

In the self-interest-driven route, traditional leaders increasingly realize that devolving their power is not contradictory to them, but is in fact in their interest and hence move towards 'Power to'.

Raghav Bahl is the poster boy of the media space in India. His broadcast network called Network18 spans print, television, film and online media. He has tie-ups with some of the largest media conglomerates in the world, including Forbes, CNN, CNBC and Viacom. In 1999, even when he could have decided otherwise, in a tiny media industry, driving a small production house without any role models to follow, Raghav made a decision to be a professionally run organization. He made a commitment to Haresh Chawla, the newly spotted executive for his company, that he would give him a free hand to build the organization. Within a few discussions, they realized that great opportunities lay in front of them, along with the many challenges.

The company should take charge of these opportunities, grow faster and should establish itself as a force to reckon with in the Indian media industry within the shortest period, they decided. However, they were also left with some stark market realities—one of them being the pace at which the media industry was changing. Every day new players were emerging, who challenged not only the existing players, but even the existing business models. The demand was on Raghav and Haresh to build a company that was nimble and agile—not just once in a while, but all the time. A few experiments down the line, they realized that it did not help their case to keep control at a central point. They needed to set up an organization that was more individual oriented, more touch-and-feel-driven than process oriented.

Raghav and Haresh laid the foundations of a company that would always be led by the 'spirit of a start-up', that would never be held down by the weight of a large central corporate structure. Quite unlike closed organizations, they framed a structure that became the guardian of their start-up culture, helping them remain lean and nimble and fight all traditionalism. Power was devolved from the leader to all levels.

Even as Network18 grew from a small television producer into a large media conglomerate, this nimbleness empowered them to stay at the top of their game. They continue running their businesses in the same informal start-up mode, where ideas come from every corner. On a continual basis, they make sure that it is the man on the field and not any overarching authority who is making decisions.

Haresh chalks out a very interesting organizational structure that has enabled Network18 to move away from the traditional 'Power over' towards 'Power to'. He compares Network18 to a series of gears connected with each other, unlike the typical top-down pyramid structure in traditional organizations. Here, the role of a leader or the top management is not that of a lever that turns these gears, but that of a lubricant which can make them work more efficiently. Ultimately, it is what is inside these gears—their individual energies—that give them the energy to perform, not some top-down structures pushing down their decisions.

In fact, Network18 even views synergies between their various companies as a hindrance, since they realize that heritage and pedigree of one can turn out to be a baggage for the other, slowing both of them down in the process. Hence, even the lubrication role of leaders is limited to the bare minimum.

Interestingly, this gear structure does not stop with the overall organizational structure, but is reflected in the running of each subsidiary. Inside every company, there are smaller gears. Free from all formal hierarchies, individuals or smaller groups take up the role of these smaller gears. Here, a business leader assumes the role of the lubricant between them.

A fast paced industry and intense competition convinced Raghav Bahl and Haresh Chawla that moving over from 'Power over' to 'Power to' and embracing Open Source leadership to traditional closed models is not a favour that they could offer their people, but in their own interests. If they continued relying on the conventional models of power, they would never be able to remain agile in a highly competitive world and would not be able to step into so many diverse areas successfully.

Though Network18 decided to embrace Open Source leadership because of external pressures, organizations also face internal pressures to devolve power. In the past, these internal pressures were in the form of unionization or strikes. However, in today's world, this has taken a different dimension, which we refer to as 'forkability'—a term borrowed from Open Source software. Forkability is the ability of anyone to take a copy of the source code and use it to start a competing project, known as a fork. In organizations outside the software realm, this forkability is about individuals in the system moving on to competition or starting up rival firms. In today's liberated environment with innumerable choices, this is for real, since people moving to the competition could undermine performance and even threaten the existence of organizations. Karl Fogel, proponent of Open Source, gives an interesting analogy. 'Imagine a king whose subjects could copy his entire kingdom at any time and move to the copy to rule as they see fit. Would not such a king govern very differently from one whose subjects were bound to stay under his rule no matter what he did?'

Haresh Chawla puts it appropriately. 'Yes, a fast changing external environment forces us to be agile. At the same time, there is also an internal pressure. If we do not devolve enough power, we would always be under the shadow of paranoia about our ideas and our people. Authority and power to people definitely help this cause.'

Second route towards a non-zero-sum leadership game: Self-interest route, where a leader moves away from closed format because he realizes that this is the only way he can combat the market realities as well as internal pressures and stay successful.

Institution-building route to Open Source leadership

Most organizations of today have taken either the self-enlightened route or the self-interest-driven route to Open Source leadership. However, at least some of these, especially the older ones, have realized a particular challenge—a challenge in relying entirely upon the enlightenment or the self-interest drive of a specific leader—because the devolution of power is still at the mercy of this leader. For example, if Jimmy Wales or Raghav Bahl so desired, they would easily be able to reverse the power back to them. The solution is a third route, 'the institution-building route', in which the power shift becomes irreversible, because it is institutionalized through formal as well as informal structures. Organizations typically embrace this route as a second step, i.e. after having come in to the Open Source fold initially through one of the first two routes.

The Indian Institute of Science (IISc), a premier science and research institute in Bangalore, recently ranked as the number one engineering and technology institute in India, even ahead of the Indian Institutes of Technology (IITs), is an example.

The spark of IISc, often referred to as the Tata Institute, was born out of a conversation between Jamsetji N. Tata, the founder of the Tata group of companies and Swami Vivekananda during a voyage to the US in 1893. IISc took shape as a unique institution; it is neither a national laboratory, which concentrates solely on research and applied work, nor a conventional university, which concerns itself mainly with teaching. It is a government institution, yet unlike many others, IISc remains extremely agile and responsive, able to innovate and introduce newer systems of imparting knowledge.

Surprisingly, Prof. P. Balram, director of IISc, a globally acknowledged scientist from the IIT and Harvard, would not attribute any of the institution's achievements to himself or even to his predecessors—who include such mighty visionaries as Sir Alfred Gibbs Bourne, Sir C.V. Raman, Sir J.C. Ghosh, Satish Dhavan and C.N.R. Rao. Instead, he credits the success to the institutions that form its foundation. 'We are less influenced by our leadership than any other normal institution. Because IISc is not a director-led institution, it does not really matter who adorns the director's chair,' he insists as he points out to the fairly open governance structures and the academic structures which run the institute.

Quite unlike other institutions, especially the ones with a long tradition and history, IISc remains open, where autonomy is guaranteed to various members as well as groups. Departments, whether administration or academic, are free to set and pursue their own goals with limited interventions from the outside. At the academic level, IISc ensures that the hierarchy is not of any relevance or importance. Irrespective of whether someone is an assistant professor or the chairman of a major department, he has the same academic status. Institutional hierarchy is in no way allowed to interfere or stifle academic matters.

For example, faculty evaluation and promotion meetings are not done by a panel from the institute, but by a neutral board of external experts drawn from all over the world.

At the same time, the institute also makes sure that these autonomous academic faculties have considerable say in any overall organizational change that could affect them. Students, likewise, are ensured their own degree of autonomy to pursue their interests, aligned just to their supervisors.

IISc embraces its Open Source leadership based on the 'institution-building route'. Rather than putting the sharing of power at the mercy of a leader, they rely on their foundational strength to create a system where the leader is just a guardian. IISc makes sure that there are enough checks and balances on the rights of this guardian that he does not transform himself to be the owner at some point. For example, the main pillar of IISc, the governing council, is comprised of representatives nominated by bodies as diverse as the government, Tata Sons, Association of Indian Universities and Technical Education Council. This diversity ensures that no one can monopolize the institution and hence it remains above everyone's vested interests.

> Third route towards a non-zero-sum leadership game: Build up a firm foundation of formal and informal structures that can institutionalize the open leadership practices above every individual.

Why leadership is not about the leader

Among the questions that traditional organizations ask about Open Source leadership, two stand out. How can a leader take one of the routes to transition from 'Power over' to 'Power to' and how should these leaders frame their organizational contexts to make sure that followers are adapting this new phenomenon?

Traditional leaders have always been attached to their power and authority, and have used them as tools to get things done in their organizations. They recognize that this 'Power over' is the source of their current management efficiencies. However, according to Prof. Balram, this attachment is a cardinal sin. He says that the first rule for a traditional leader to follow, if he is interested in moving towards Open Source leadership, is the 'Rule of Detachment', where the leader takes a detached interest towards his organization. This detachment does not mean that the leader is not interested in the activities of the organization. He is interested and involved, as much as he always was. However, this interest is devoid of any craving for the enlargement of power because a leader can never truly devolve if he competes with his people. A detached leader keeps the interest of his organization at the highest level, even at times when it happens to go against his own interest. In other words, 'purpose over self'.

However, any meaningful level of detachment is not easy, because human beings as a species are physiologically wired to develop an attachment to the things around us. Researchers at Ohio State University and Illinois State University recently reported a finding that simply touching a coffee cup for a few seconds could create a personal attachment to it. The amazing part of this study is that people can become almost immediately attached to something as insignificant as a mug,' wrote the study's lead author, James Wolf, in the journal *Judgment and Decision Making*. 'By simply touching the mug and feeling it in their hands, many people begin to feel like the mug is, in fact, their mug. Once they begin to feel it is theirs, they are willing to go to greater lengths to keep it.'

If that is how we react to something as trivial as a cup for our morning java, how is a leader to resist taking on all the power and authority of their position as a personal possession? How can someone at the top possibly practise the art of detachment?

Prof. Balram steps in here again with a solution, drawing from his experience at the IISc. 'In the IISc there is a pre-entered custom that the director of the institute must be a professor from the institute. If someone comes from the outside, he must take up professorship first and only then would the head position be offered to him. From a leadership perspective, this means that a leader has his own wider interests beyond administration; an alternate (*sic*) interest that could balance his role at the institute. So, beyond all the positions that he adorns, he might be a distinguished researcher, who has a laboratory to go to and a group of students to interact with. This diversified interest acts as a grounding factor, sparking off a detachment, making sure that the leader has no time to drive a personal agenda. With an alternate (*sic*) passion, a leader no longer needs to spend all his time worrying about how to hoard more power.'

First idea to encourage transition from 'Power over' to 'Power to': Practise the art of detachment. Engage in an alternate passion.

Prof. Balram's reasoning is simple: if a leader continues to think that his 'power' is the centre point of his organization, or the basis of the respect that he commands, it would be extremely difficult to convince him to dilute any of this power. But, if he has an alternative interest that drives him, he would no longer see his role as a top-down authoritarian decision maker, but as an organizational facilitator who welcomes divergent views as a way to ease the pressure on him rather than as a threat. Allison Garrett, vice-president of academic affairs at Oklahoma Christian University, writes about an interesting rule that could complement Prof. Balram's thinking. She refers to this rule as 'Nose in, Fingers out', meaning leaders are supposed to be nosey, but they are not supposed to interfere and take over all the decision making themselves, nor are they supposed to overturn others' decisions to their advantage. 'Open leaders do not make decisions—they simply help their people to make better decisions. To do this, they listen well, ask probing questions and push for more information. Then, when they see the prevailing wisdom surface, they communicate those decisions more fruitfully.'

Second idea to encourage transition from 'Power over' to 'Power to': Be nosey, but do not put your fingers in.

Another interesting concept, borrowed from the Open Source software community is 'Last word leader, instead of first'. Traditional leaders thrive on first word—where every idea originates from the leader and flows down from there. Unfortunately, this sends in two messages for the organization—the leader has better skills than everyone else, and he is the only one who has the authority to push ideas down. However, in order to transition from 'Power over' to 'Power to', leaders have to give up their right as the originator of ideas. A leader indeed might have superior skills; nevertheless, 'as a last word, instead of first', he takes on a self-imposed restraint to step in only when his presence is required. He gives up his right to speak so that the rest of them can find their voice.

Different from the first word, where superior skills are important for a leader, in the case of last word an overall sense is what is required—not necessarily the ability to produce on demand but an ability to encourage and recognize good ideas. Here, a leader takes up the role of filtering out bad ideas and forming the good ideas into a coherent whole. A good way to understand this difference is by contrasting a military commander—an authoritarian—to that of an arbitrator who does not actually make the decisions, but instead lets things work themselves out through discussions and experimentation.

However, this does not mean that Open Source Leaders do not actively participate in any discussions. In fact, in many Open Source leadership organizations, they do. However, not as leaders or as participants, but as mere observers: helping to shift the context in which people gather, naming the debate through powerful questions, and listening rather than providing answers. It is only when it is clear that no consensus can be reached, or that the group genuinely demands the leader's interference, do they step in—as the last word.

> Third idea to encourage transition from 'Power over' to 'Power to': Practise to be a 'Last-word leader' and not a 'First-word one'.

So, what happens if the leader has an opposing view to that which has been reached by consensus? For example, in Open Source software development, there are several instances where many solutions arrived at by the community were against the thoughts of Linus Torvalds, the founder. Yet, he did accept, sometimes even grudgingly, what was wanted by the majority. Because he realized that the existence of his Open Source community itself depended upon his deliberate constraining of his authority. At the same time, in case of issues that were close to his heart, which he felt were important to the foundational set-up, he debated passionately and strived to bring them around to his point; the operative word over here being 'strive' not force.

According to Linus, even in such cases, one of the cardinal mistakes to be avoided is taking sides that might splinter his followers. 'I would much rather have fifteen people arguing about something than fifteen people splitting into two camps, each side convinced it is right and not talking to the other,' he says in an interview with *Wired Magazine*. In fact, often when things were on the verge of getting messy, he would consciously avoid making a decision, allowing time for feelings to dissipate. 'Eventually, some obvious solution would emerge or the issue would just fade away,' he says.

Haresh Chawla suggests that in Network18, in case of differences of opinions, Raghav Bahl would share his view with their people. Nonetheless, it was still up to the people whether they should accept it or not, because irrespective of whether they accepted or not, the success or failure of the decision would still rest with them. 'Here is my point of view, but at the end of the day the call is yours,' is the overall attitude.

Fourth idea to encourage transition from 'Power over' to 'Power to': Abstain from taking sides, even on issues close to your heart.

As leaders move towards 'Power to' from 'Power over' they have to give up many of the conventional practices and thinking they are used to, for example, the sheer definition of power. In traditional organizations, power is everything that defines a leader's position. The more power he has, the better he is. But in Open Source leadership, the focus shifts to how the leader is sharing his power, and how he is adapting to his new-found role. His position is no longer defined by the authority he holds, but the influence that he has without it.

However, leaders are not the only set of people whose power

is affected as Open Source leadership takes shape. Subordinates are another important party, who have until now, been taking all the authority over them as granted. Surprisingly, they have their own incentives to remain in this state. Which is primarily the cost attached to 'power'—the cost of being accountable. In the current organizational context, where leaders hold all the power, subordinates are absolved of authorities and hence accountabilities. They can afford to be passive and non-responsive. Nevertheless, the backbone of Open Source leadership is increased power and hence increased accountabilities from people at all levels. Everyone has to be brought together in such a way that no one shuns or shirks. Which brings us to the next important question—how can leaders shift the organizational context in such a way that people across their organization have an incentive to embrace Open Source leadership?

How Open Source Leaders are bribing their people to be leaders

Steven Levitt, celebrated author of *Freakanomics*, in his article 'Why Vote?', narrates a case study of voting behaviour in Switzerland. He says, though the Swiss love to vote, the participation declined over years. Authorities speculated that this could be because of the cost associated with the time and efforts spend on voting and hence thought up an interesting initiative—an initiative that would lower the cost of casting the vote significantly—postal ballot. Here, every eligible Swiss citizen would receive a ballot in the post, which could then be completed and returned. The authorities presumed that the decline would now be arrested. Ironically, the voter turnout nosedived, especially in small towns, instead of going up. But why?

Levitt writes that the culprit was misjudging the real incentives behind voting. The authorities thought that saving their citizens from the effort of tromping to the polls during a rainstorm could be the real incentive. But they were wrong, since for Swiss voters, the real incentive was not affecting the election outcome (which anyway you cannot, since odds that one person's vote would actually affect the election outcome are really slim), but a sense of civic duty, where they would be perceived as good citizens. When poll-voting was the only option, they had a motivation for being 'seen' handing in the vote—hope for social esteem, benefits from being perceived as a cooperator or just the avoidance of informal sanctions. In small communities, where everyone knew everyone else, the incentive from this adherence to social norm was particularly high. However, quite contrary to what authorities thought, the postal ballot took away this incentive, leading to plummeting in voting percentage.

In the short term, organizational evolution towards Open Source leadership could be stymied by a lack of correct belief systems and incentive structures, like what happened in the case of the Swiss authorities. Leaders again have a role to play here. They play a role in devising the correct incentive structures that can encourage their people to increasingly come out of their comfort zones, to embrace bigger responsibilities.

> People down the ladder will embrace Open Source leadership, only if given the right incentives.

Surprisingly, these incentives need not be monetary, as we have all been made to believe. In his book, *Punished by Rewards*, author Alfie Kohn says that monetary rewards can be most damaging at times, since they suggest to our inner minds that we are doing the task for a reward rather than the enjoyment of it. Open Source leadership realizes this—that many a time, the reward is the job itself. If a leader can make a task look intrinsically motivating, there need not be any better incentive for people to move towards the goal. Linus Torvalds, for instance, advocates fun as a powerful incentive among his hacker community. He believes that the huge programmer base is a result of this incentive, where people are allowed to discover what they really like doing and then allowing them to do it for the love of it, without any external pressure. As the influence of the Linux community is growing, the business world is learning a surprising lesson: that right incentives could drive people to do things and produce results that often surpass those working for money.

How the Open Source leadership model is eliminating the traditional role of a leader

Swamy Pragyapath met 'guru of joy' Sri Sri Ravi Shankar, the founder of the Art of Living Foundation—an Open Source leadership, educational and humanitarian non- profit organization with a presence in over 140 countries—fifteen years ago, while he was an engineering student at the IIT, Mumbai. Being from one of the most elite educational institutes, it was not surprising that he had already received several coveted job offers. However, those did not appeal to him, since a few days at the Art of Living ashram had already changed his perspective about work.

In our traditional organizations, like the ones Pragyapath got his offers from, work and fun are clearly demarcated through ingeniously devised systems. Fixed office hours is one of them, where the idea is that if you cannot make people work, you can at least prevent them from having fun. Here, the assumption is that when employees are restricted in their office building for certain fixed hours a day, and are forbidden from non-work activities, they must be working. Though this assumption looks excellent in theory, in practice this falls flat. Employees spend a lot of their time in a no-man's land, where they are neither working nor having fun.

However, work and fun need not be separate, and fun could be a powerful way to let people work, realized Pragyapath after his short stint at the ashram. So, it was not surprising, even for himself, that he decided to accept an invite from his guruji, Sri Sri, to join the ashram, though there were no commitments of fat salaries or great career prospects. Like in the case of Linux programmers, in the Art of Living Foundation also people work long hours and take up responsibilities, even outside their regular realms, not because they are forced, but because they are enjoying themselves.

First idea to let people embrace larger accountabilities of Open Source leadership:
Make the job itself rewarding. Make responsibilities fun rather than drab.

Creating enjoyment in the workplace is a powerful incentive for people to take up new responsibilities of Open Source leadership. So is adherence to a larger cause. People in traditional organizations are almost always left to feel like 'cogs in the giant wheel', with no idea about the larger cause or the larger project that they belong to. They are always coding, data crunching or selling mindlessly. A larger cause can make people feel larger than life and passionate, helping them to put into perspective their work. Affiliation to a greater vision can make them willing to do things for the good of the whole, even when they do not benefit personally.

'With a vision of "Making life a celebration", Art of Living combines passion and adherence to a larger cause effectively,' suggests Pragyapath.

'Guruji keeps telling us that the world is one family and hence we need to reach out Art of Living to everyone. We need to make life a celebration; not just in the ashram, but also for all other life on this planet. As we go about our daily activities, we know that we are helping in building a peaceful world. Even as we are working during the wee hours of the day in the remotest parts of the world, amidst deep dangers, we know that we are doing the right thing, that we are giving back to our society to build a better world. And that keeps us going.'

Second idea to let people embrace larger accountabilities of Open Source leadership:
Have a larger cause that can make people feel larger than life.

Dr Devi Shetty, India's most famous heart surgeon and the founder of Narayana Hrudayalaya, a multi-specialty hospital in Bangalore, echoes the same sentiments as he strives towards building Open

Source leadership in the world of medical practice. Dr Shetty dreams of a world where cardiac surgery would be affordable to everyone, including the poorest of the poor. He is not just dreaming, but also doing, through a carefully thought-out and well-devised two-pronged plan. In the first prong, he is building health cities across the nation, where integrated medical facilities would be provided to the needy at affordable costs. In the second, he has rolled out a 'micro health plan' called 'Yashaswini'. At twenty cents a month, and covering more than three million poor farmers, with almost 100,000 operations in the last four years, this unique health insurance scheme is possibly the world's largest and cheapest.

However, Dr Shetty has already realized that the success of such ambitious and impacting programmes cannot become successful just by relying on the conventional ways of doing things. 'Just my willingness to devolve power would not help us achieve our dream. Others should be equally willing to take up responsibilities and be accountable. However, things are even more complicated in the medical profession. One, to take charge of such a large vision, we need people who are not only brilliant in the medical profession, but also good in creating and managing systems. And second, most health care professionals are stuck in the current system where things are managed in ways that are far from ideal. Many health care professionals behave awkwardly, because most of them are working in a manner that they do not enjoy. So, my whole concept is based on attracting talented doctors, creating a platform where they can work and enjoy, where they can awaken their basic good instincts, where they are willing to share and learn together.'

To create the right incentive system for getting people ready for 'Power to' and in turn for Open Source leadership, Dr Shetty has devised a unique mechanism—to run hospitals like academic institutions, almost like 'gurukuls' (a traditional residential and open learning system in India)—in letter as well as in spirit. The base of these gurukuls is comprised of young surgeons, who are fresh graduates out of medical colleges. The mission of the gurukul is to train these youngsters under the best senior surgeons, in the most rigorous manner, so that they would be as good as the seniors in about five years or so. But there is a negative incentive in this for the seniors. If junior surgeons would be as good as they are in five years, it also holds a threat of them being surpassed in no time—after all juniors have the advantage of more time with them, have better understanding of the latest methodologies and are taught by some of the brilliant senior minds.

So, why should these star senior doctors devote their time and attention to training a bunch of newcomers who would eventually overtake them? Here, we should also consider the fact that these seniors have reached the highest levels in their profession, through absolute hard work, of more than twenty hours a day, every day. Through their tough journey, they have accumulated eccentricities, egos and a highly competitive spirit, even ready to tear each other apart. In short, it would take a really powerful incentive system to get these seniors to part with all the experience that they have acquired over the years.

Dr Shetty says that the beauty of the gurukul system is that it offers seniors as well as juniors just the right set of incentives. For a senior, the system offers an opportunity to create his own fan following in the juniors that he has empowered, providing him a signalling incentive in terms of increased status in his circle. The better he empowers his juniors, the more is the recognition that he can boast of among his highly competitive peers: 'You know, I trained the world-famous surgeon Dr X.' At the same time, for a junior, the gurukul offers the incentive of growing faster and becoming a star himself. The more he pays attention, the faster he would grow to be a star senior.

The ultimate advantage is of course, for the institution. It keeps growing, with minimum friction between old stars and newer stars, making Dr Shetty's gurukul system a great example of true Open Source leadership and how organizations can offer the right

incentive systems so that people—leaders as well as subordinates—
make their transition from 'Power over' to 'Power to'.

> **Third idea to let people embrace larger accountabilities of Open Source leadership:**
> **Let people assume greater accountabilities for their own sake rather than for**
> **any others.**

HCL Technologies, which *Time* magazine once referred to as 'an
intellectual clean room where its employees could imagine endless
possibilities', and which was the subject of a Harvard Business School
case study, is one of India's largest IT companies, headquartered in
New Delhi. HCL, another Open Source leadership organization,
has a unique concept, 'Employee First Customer Second', which
they consider the cornerstone of their philosophy. They treat their
employees to be the most important asset, compared to even their
customers—conventionally thought to be the real interest of the
stakeholders. At HCL, every single practice focuses on moving
from the traditional 'Power over' to 'Power to', where power is
developed and shared in a collective manner, striving to stimulate
performances of each other. Here, responsibilities are not always
given, but taken, sometimes even by pushing your manager out, by
acquiring his competencies and growing into his position.

HCL believes that intrinsic motivation factors, like the one we
saw in the case of Dr Shetty's gurukul system, is just not enough.
'There should be explicit extrinsic incentive systems too, else most
people would be too complacent to take up bigger responsibilities,'
says Anand Pillai, global head for Talent Transformation and
Intrapreneurship Development at HCL. 'Given an opportunity,
every manager would like to create his own comfort zone in the
organization. However, at HCL this would come at a cost, because
no person would be eligible for promotions, unless he has trained
other people in the organization to do his job better than he. In
fact, we have devised a structure in such a way that it is better for
people to train than not train.

'However, the managerial ladder is not the only place where employees want to be. In any organization, we find people who have great ideas and who want to build those things by remaining in the safety of their organizations, rather than striking it out on their own. All they want is support from their leaders. More often than not, traditional organizations would not let them—because of systems, bureaucracies or just plain insecurities of the leader. At HCL, if a manager is able to train another person into his role, he would not only have a bigger role in the organization, but also would be allowed to invest a part of his time to pursue projects of his choice, even outside his regular profile. He would have his freedom, could engage in his real interests, and the organization would offer him support even in terms of resources,' concludes Anand Pillai.

> Fourth idea to let people embrace larger accountabilities of Open Source leadership: Build your organizational structure itself around the incentives that can enable people to assume higher responsibilities, rather than the other way round.

Those of us who are used to the conventional ways of doing things, can accuse Open Source leadership of being a utopian dream. They cannot be blamed, because to the naked eye, it appears to be so. We are convinced that the way things are done currently is the right way. This is primarily because we are comfortable with it, especially with the way power is defined between leaders and subordinates. Traditional leaders are comfortable with the way they 'Power over' their subordinates. They refuse to share any of it, citing that this is important for the success of the organization. Followers, at the same time, treat this monopoly of power by leaders as an excuse to shun accountabilities. However, the right incentives can really convert this utopian dream into a reality. Well-defined incentives, for leaders and subordinates alike, can break down conventional thinking and can move us towards 'Power to' and Open Source leadership—the evolutionarily stable form that would survive in the future.

3

A Case for Endless Office Gossiping
Open Source Leadership Builds and Nurtures Social Capital as an Alternative to Traditional Management Mechanisms

In this section:
- How organizational processes—intended for easier coordination and faster response—produce the opposite result
- Why new age leaders are destroying the same hierarchies that they painfully built up
- Why coffee table conversations and prolonged lunch breaks produce better results in improving organizational productivity

How organizational processes—intended for easier coordination and faster response—produce the opposite result

The main objective of any organization is coordinating the actions of a group of individuals to attain a certain goal. However, coordination does not happen automatically, but requires some efforts, since individuals do not collaborate on their own, especially on goals that are outside their immediate purview. Initially, before the arrival of classical Taylorism, this coordination was achieved through an abundant stock of 'social capital'—the level of trust and goodwill between individuals and their communities, established through the informal social interactions between them. People were able to easily work together in the professional atmosphere because they knew each other in their personal spheres.

However, once management became a formal science, thinkers assumed that modern companies progressively should replace social capital with formal systems like management policies, hierarchies and bureaucratic rules. As businesses started becoming more complex by the day, they insisted that the relationship between the organization and its people was purely contractual. According to them, the organization's role is to merely set up the correct system, and need not extend beyond that in any manner. Once the correct system is in place, people will find their own interest to take the best possible actions and the organization as a whole will attain higher levels of efficiency.

In the shorter term, this contractual arrangement worked very well, especially in industrial environments, where it added more predictability to the business operations. Planning, organizing, staffing, reviewing, budgeting—everything was possible with a greater level of control for the top management. However, it would not be without its own challenges. Primary among them was a phenomenon called 'transaction cost'—a term that became most widely known through economist Oliver E. Williamson's work. Often known as coordination cost, it is the cost of all the information processing and monitoring necessary to coordinate the work of people in an organization, primarily because in the absence of social capital people started considering their professional conduct as nothing but a contract and hence cooperated only when the organization was willing to bear the cost. For the company, this meant increased transaction costs, which came in several shades—information costs to locate the right resources to carry out tasks, reward costs to incentivize people to work towards specified actions, monitoring costs to make sure that people are not shirking the responsibilities, and enforcement costs to take appropriate action, if anyone defects.

Rigidity and unresponsiveness of contracts was yet another challenge of formal coordination mechanisms. Since no contract could possibly specify every contingency that may arise between the parties, most had to just presuppose a certain amount of goodwill that would prevent the parties from taking advantage of unforeseen loopholes. Contracts that did seek to specify all contingencies ended up being very inflexible and costly to enforce, resulting in further inefficiencies. For example, many complex services are very costly to monitor and are better controlled through internalized professional standards than through formal monitoring mechanisms. A highly educated software engineer often knows much more about his own productivity than his supervisor; procurement is often more efficient when left to the judgement of an experienced procurement officer, rather than being done 'by the book'. In fact a number of empirical studies even suggest that high technology R&D is often dependent on the informal exchange of intellectual property rights, simply because formal exchange would entail excessive transaction costs and slow down the speed of interchange.

Open Source leadership has woken up to the fact that modern management techniques—intended for easier coordination and faster response—at times produce just the opposite result by imposing various forms of transaction costs and rigid and unresponsive structures. They have realized that though it appeared in today's complex and technologically sophisticated world that social capital might not be of much use, in truth it remains as relevant as in pre-Taylorian times.

Why new age leaders are destroying the same hierarchies that they painfully built up

Fog Creek Software is a US-based software company specializing in project management tools. Apart from some of the wonderful tools this company has created, it is also known for its unique office spaces, with a goal to make the best programming workspace possible. Its first large office, in midtown Manhattan, was custom-designed and featured angled walls and a window next to each of them, to allow its programmers redemption from the typical cubicle farms.

Joel Spolsky, the founder and CEO, once wrote about an incident that happened during their initial days in the new office. Visitors to the company were surprised to see two youngsters walking around with drills in hand, climbing ladders and hanging blinds in all the programmers' offices. And the reason for surprise was not that the work was going on after everyone had moved in but because one of the chaps happened to be Joel, while the other was Michael Pryor, the CFO of the company.

Joel writes that this task, which could have taken any half-skilled handyman a few hours, and a couple of thousand dollars, ended up consuming more than two days. Added to that was the top management time which they could have very well spent in doing something more valuable, or something less tedious. So why were these two chaps, the CEO and the CFO of the company insistent on doing the low task of hanging window blinds themselves? They could have called a handyman, or they could have at least assigned this task to a junior member!

It is in fact easy for any CEO to think that he is the most valuable person in the company, that his time and efforts are more precious that anyone else's in the organization. Whether this is true or not, this thinking erects a barrier between the leader and his people—a barrier that could stand in the way of open social interactions. Joel writes that through their seemingly silly gesture of hanging window blinds, they were trying to break down this barrier in their company. By getting out there and dirtying their hands, they managed to send out a message that the CEO was not separated from his people, either through his position, or through the work which he does.

In any organization, there are two kinds of relationships that build up social capital between its members—horizontal and vertical. Horizontal relationships are those that are formed between members who can connect to each other on a more or less equal level—in terms of positions, designations or social status. But vertical relationships—like the one which we have seen in the case of Joel and his team, are the ties between unequals in the organizational hierarchy—between the higher-ups and lower-downs. As would be expected, it is much easier to nurture horizontal relationships compared to vertical ones, since vertical ones always tend to be coloured with hues of authority and power. Communications in vertical relationships are typically reserved, measured, and calculated so that they signal and reiterate positions. Exchanges in vertical relationships again serve hierarchies—they preserve the privileged positions at the upper level, and offer advantages to the lower level to serve the higher levels.

Since relationships are hierarchy-driven, there are always risks and insecurities associated with trying to reach out and build informal ties between levels. While doing so, top levels tend to lose their authority and lower levels tend to lose their security—and hence are a difficult task. Though several leaders approach open-door policies and employee participation with sincerity, it is almost always met with cynicism, sarcasm and ambivalence from all parts of the hierarchy, primarily because of these insecurities. At the same time, if an organization succeeds in enabling its vertical ties to attain the informality and warmth of horizontal relations, there would truly be a transformation in the way the organization views openness, collaboration and dedication.

Often, the best way to build social capital in the vertical ties is by taking a leaf out of Joel's book—by physically getting out there and symbolically breaking down any barriers that could stand in the way of open interactions. Many a time, the greatest obstacle to getting the people to relate to a leader is the leader himself, who sits in his impermeable glass house as the lord high of everything. Of course, the barriers could be broken down by the people also, but except in extreme cases this do not happen, primarily because down the hierarchy insecurities tend to be more. There is much to lose, though there could also be something to gain. But immediate losses weigh over a distant gain. Hence, it almost always comes down to the leader to tear down the obstacles.

Being another youngster full of cynicism, Pragyapath might not have been too important for Sri Sri Ravi Shankar in his scheme of things at the Art of Living Ashram. Yet, Sri Sri left no stone unturned. Pragyapath says, 'The first time I ever met up with guruji something dropped in me. I cannot put it into words. But some barrier, probably it could have been a wall of scepticism, just vanished. Not because I was lost in a devotional atmosphere, but because guruji made an effort to sit with me, listen to my questions and ever so patiently answer me. Even as people were thronging from all sides to meet up with him, he made it feel as if I were the only person who mattered to him. He got me committed through this single gesture of reaching out to me.'

He continues, 'Interestingly, this reaching out process was not limited to the first meeting. Guruji continued doing so on a constant and continuous basis. The greatest weapon he uses for breaking down the barriers around is by being a role model. He advises us on many things, and we listen, but when we see him practising it, we connect at a deeper level. We connect in a way that we would never forget.

'It is more than fifteen years since I came to this ashram. It was much smaller then. This place was almost a far-flung corner outside Bangalore, with much less greenery than you see now,' continues Pragyapath pointing out to the lush greenery. 'Facilities were sparse. In fact, I remember a specific incident distinctly—a time when there was a severe water shortage. All of us at the ashram were outside fetching water so that all could cook, wash and clean. As I was new in the ashram, I expected guruji, our leader, to be inside the ashram meditating, leaving others to take care of the chores. However, I was surprised when I saw him along with us, filling water in buckets and carrying it across. He used those seemingly drab moments to be with us, to share our burdens. We knew that he was with us, one among us. That broke all the barriers.

'Even today guruji never loses an opportunity to be with his people. Be it casual conversations or satsangs (a spiritual discourse or sacred gathering), he creates this feeling that he is everywhere in the campus for everyone. The greatest motivation or fear in all of us as we do some of those monotonous jobs—be it allocating rooms to our participants, or making sure facilities are taken care of—is the fact that if we don't do it, guruji would do it himself.'

Step one to break the hierarchy barriers: Walk the talk. Be a role model.

Being a role model definitely helps in cutting across hierarchies to build social capital, because that helps people to relate to the leader as one of their own. Meanwhile, there is another simple step which open leaders rely on to produce a quick stock of social capital—loving and caring for their people. John Maxwell says, 'You cannot lead your people until you can love them.' Though it sounds simple, most leaders do not really understand the depth of this statement, because respect as an attribute, though always expected as a right by the organizational leaders, is seldom reciprocated. Most leaders do not realize that it is this misplaced perception of respect, as a one-way street, that is probably the biggest hurdle in the way of better vertical ties.

David Burns, a professor of psychiatry and behavioural sciences writes, 'The biggest mistake you can make is to keep expecting due respect and priority to your ideas and feelings, without any care for others. Being in a leadership position, you might even think that you are getting it, but it need not be true, since this could be just an external exhibition prompted by other factors like fear or greed. Leaders need to realize that what most people really want is the same set of values that they expect—to be listened to, respected and understood. The moment people see that they are being understood, they become more motivated to understand your point of view.'

After an international Test debut at Lord's in 1996, Sourav Ganguly, whom Geoffery Boycott, one of the legends of the cricketing world, referred to as 'the prince of Calcutta', took over as the captain of Indian cricket team in the year 2000. However, he inherited a team that had nothing to feel proud about. The team was reeling under one of its lowest phases—with a series loss to both Australia and South Africa. Cricket has always been a craze in India, but cricketing as a profession was very different and a difficult proposition. Getting into the national team was definitely a big challenge, but once you managed to get inside, the challenges just grew bigger. The team was stranded in various gulfs—between the captain and the players, seniors and juniors, between players of different regions. The Indian cricket team, which Ganguly took over, consisted more of eleven distinct individuals rather than a united team. Trust, interactions and social capital were at its worst. And Ganguly probably would have been the worst person to handle such a job—quiet, almost aloof and often branded as egoistic. In fact, he was notorious for his attitude problems and lack of respect for the senior players.

However, Ganguly took over the reins with a firm decision to change the rules of the game that he was used to, and all others were also used to in India. The change was indeed nothing short of miraculous. From a soggy, also ran, and always-apologetic-to-win team, India started turning around to a team that spelled aggression, innovation and hunger to win. From a bunch of aimless individuals who were focused on regionalism and self-glorification, there were glimpses of teamwork and selfless collaboration, and a true transformation towards Open Source leadership started. And most importantly, the team started winning games. Under Ganguly's stewardship India played forty-nine test matches, winning twenty-one of those, including twelve of them outside India—all three figures records of sorts. He led the team to their first series wins in both Tests and One-Day Internationals in Pakistan, a feat that had eluded India for over fifty years. He led India to victory over Steve Waugh's Australia in the 2001 Border–Gavaskar trophy and to the finals of the 2003 World Cup, considered to be among the finest moments in Indian cricket history.

Sachin Tendulkar, one of the greatest batsmen the world has seen, remembered this in a newspaper interview after a historic win in New Zealand in 2009.

'The winning streak that the Indian cricket team is going through now started in Zimbabwe, our breakthrough victory in 2001. Though India lost the next Test, it showed us that we could do it. We went to the West Indies immediately after that. We won a Test there. Then in England, South Africa and Australia. We made an impact wherever we went after that. We just needed the team to fall in place along with a good break and we got that under the captaincy of Ganguly. We are just continuing that winning streak.'

But how did he do it? 'I was made the captain as the team was passing through one of the toughest stages. In the early stages, I did not believe that such a thing could happen but it soon became difficult to deny that. I had to get my team together again. Cricket is such a big sport that we could not afford to break down,' said Ganguly in an interview to a newspaper.

'Captaining India has never been easy. There is so much pressure, media presence and innumerable demands—on the field and off it too. But I was not afraid to experiment and find out my own way of leading the team,' he says, explaining how he drove the team to merge seamlessly into a spirited unit. 'I let the boys free. I wanted to lead a bunch of fighters. I was very close to a lot of them and they enjoyed my trust. They knew that I was a man who would not hurt anyone from behind. I did lose my temper when I did not see the boys putting in their effort. I did not mind non-performance with effort . . . But all my complaints and anger would finish on the field. Off it, my reactions were different.'

Harbhajan Singh, lovingly known as Bhajji, made his Test and One-Day International cricket debuts in early 1998, but his career was initially beset by investigations into the legality of his bowling action and disciplinary incidents that raised the ire of cricket authorities. However in 2001, Harbhajan's career was resuscitated after Ganguly called for his inclusion in the team for the Border–Gavaskar Trophy, a series that India went on to win where Harbhajan established himself as the team's leading spinner by taking thirty-two wickets and becoming the first Indian bowler to take a hat-trick in Test cricket. There could be no one better than Harbhajan to comment about the foundations on which Ganguly built this remarkable team.

'Sourav Ganguly is like my brother, in fact is my brother,' says Bhajji. 'The most remarkable thing about Sourav is that he brought back the basic respect in the Indian cricket team. As an individual, I thought I was treated very shabbily during some of the earlier incidents in my cricketing life. Sourav changed my perceptions, even as I went through some of the toughest times. The situation was such that my chances were very slim in playing for India again. Sourav needed a spinner for the Australian team and he instinctively knew that I could be his man, in spite of my bad spell. And from that moment, I knew that I would do anything for him. That spirit enabled me to take thirty-two wickets which eventually got me "The Man of the Series". Sourav trusted in me, and he respected me for that. And that changed my life.

'And I was not an exception,' continues Bhajji. 'He behaved the same way to everyone in the team. He was the captain and he could do whatever he wanted to do. In fact that was the way things were in the team. But he was never like that. Though we were juniors, he never made us feel that way. In fact, he used to go to any extent to make us feel important under him. He would come to us and talk to us all the time—about the match, about the team and even about personal matters. That simple act changed our perspectives.

'Until that time our perspective was that the entire responsibility of the team was with the seniors—scoring runs, taking wickets, taking risks. But as Sourav started talking to us and started taking our suggestions, we suddenly realized that the responsibility was equally on us. He not only allowed us to speak out in the team meetings, but even asked us to experiment and take ownership of those experiments. He gave us the confidence to even take up more responsibility from our seniors.

'It is rather simple. When a captain does so much for you, it becomes our responsibility to perform and win the match. That is probably the least that we could do.'

Step two to break the hierarchy barriers: Respect your people, even in areas that they least expect.

However, respect does not get translated into social capital, if people do not see the leader walking the talk, where a leader continuously and repeatedly confirms the impressions that they have formed about him. In other words, trust develops from repeated experiences that the leader provides for his people.

Ashish Nehra debuted in the One-Day International scenario in the year 2001 under Sourav Ganguly. He was a part of the Indian dream run in the World Cup 2003 in South Africa. Though he made a good start, he failed to cement his place in the Indian team primarily due to his injuries. He has great wisdom to offer, 'Players trusting the captain starts from captain trusting the players. Players can smell this trust, as they see their captain backing them, based only on their potential, beyond all politics and favouritism.

'In India cricket is a religion, and hence pressure on players is very high. They can easily go in to a negative frame of mind, if they go through a two- or three-innings failure. Imagine my plight when I got injured after a good spell and could not play for eighteen months or so,' Ashish wonders. 'I was literally shattered. However, Sourav was always there to support me. He encouraged me to play a good season of domestic cricket so that he could ensure my comeback into the team. I knew I could trust him because he was with me not just in good times, but also in bad times, not just in words but also in deeds.'

Bhajji adds on to this, 'If you are my captain and if you come up to me and say, "Listen, I will make sure that you bowl so many overs, in return I want you to make sure you too get these number of wickets," how can you ever not put your heart and soul into achieving it. However, that commitment also has to do with the realization that it is not about a ruthless business deal. He genuinely cares about me as a person. He often had meals with me and enquired about my family. It touched a chord there.'

According to Ramesh Rao, the camp coordinator of the National Cricket Academy in Bangalore, the most defining quality of Sourav Ganguly is that he would never hurt any of the boys, even when they committed unintentional mistakes like throwing away a precious wicket or runs that could have saved the game. Ramesh comments, 'Sourav always dealt with each player with utmost care, as if the player was always more important than the match. If a match was lost because of a person, he would almost always be the first person who would walk up to him, put his hands around his shoulders, to console him that it was just another bad day. At the same time, after the emotions had died down, he would sit with the boys and analyse the mistakes, and how they could be corrected.'

Ashish continues on the same note, 'Sourav would always call you up even when you were off the field to discuss team strategies. He would listen to everybody. But that does not mean that he would automatically take your suggestions because ultimately cricket is also a game of instincts. Sometimes, he would take his decisions based on the realities of the field. Nevertheless, if Sourav did not implement any of the suggestions, he almost always used to give that player an explanation.'

Vijaya Menon, who was earlier the head of marketing at Air Deccan (this pioneering low-cost airline in India was later bought over by Kingfisher Airlines and renamed Kingfisher Red), reflects the same sentiments as she talks about what made the employees trust Captain Gopinath, the founder leader of the company. She says, 'He need not have done certain things for us, but yet he did them, though some of them required him to go out of his way. He always used to roam around and ask people how things were going on. People knew that he genuinely cared for us. That was the foundation of our trust.

'Trust also derives out of how the leader is engaging you.' Vijaya continues, 'Let me give you an example. When the merger between Kingfisher and Air Deccan was announced, for Kingfisher it was the chairman Vijay Mallya's moments. But then there was Captain Gopi, who was looking around to find out if we were there, and whether we were comfortable. He made us feel that we were special, though we had nothing really to do with the moment as such. Captain Gopi is able to go across and cut across in order to create an open organization.'

> Step three to break the hierarchy barriers: Repeatedly confirm the impressions that your people have formed about you. Make them trust you.

Having laid a foundation of respect and trust, relationships bloom across vertical ties as the leader and his people share common experiences. In fact, the shared experiences take the respect and trust to the next level, helping people to work alongside with the leader, truly building Open Source leadership.

Shared experiences cut across vertical ties in two ways. First, it helps identify and acknowledge similarities across hierarchies. Interestingly, these similarities need not be professionally based ones like skills or capabilities. In fact subtler ones like emotions, feelings, etc. can help build stronger bonds. Second, it also helps in understanding and appreciating differences between individuals—those unique gifts and abilities that most of the time get lost in organizational rigmarole. Recognizing these and appreciating them can help in ironing out differences of opinion as well as understanding differing perspectives.

'We had 3,000 employees on the rolls and another 5,000 contract staff when we sold off,' Vijaya says. 'But we never had the budget to entertain, while in all the rest of the competition airlines, there were several get-together parties. We could never afford any of those. Yet, we had one of the least attrition levels and one of the best working cultures. Those were not created by any artificial environments like office parties, but the real experience of working together—through good times and a lot of bad times.'

Ashish Nehra says, 'I think, when we talk about Sourav's leadership, the first thing that comes to mind is that he was very relaxed with the boys. He used to allow you to play your game and at the same time kept everything simple. He never used to complicate things.' Some captains even dictate what players should be doing off the field. But Sourav was never like that. He never used to do things just to prove a point. But at the same time he would go out of the way to make sure that we were comfortable with him, not just while playing, even otherwise. If you wanted to just sit and chat in the dressing room, you could, or you could sleep, or you could even blast your music. We were free to party or free to just go out and meet up with our girlfriends. He would never stop someone, as long as he was confident that together we were doing well. That created an atmosphere where we could not just relate to our captain, but could share our experiences together, not just as players, but as friends.'

> Step four to break the hierarchy barriers: Let trust be reiterated and transformed into results through shared experiences.

John Maxwell sums up well. 'Few things will pay you bigger dividends than the time and trouble you take to understand your people and be one of them. Almost nothing will add more to your stature as a leader and as a person. Nothing will give you greater satisfaction or bring you more happiness.'

Why coffee table conversations and prolonged lunch breaks produce better results in improving organizational productivity

'There is no well-equipped gym. There are no offices—corner, nice or otherwise. There are no windows. There are no well-stocked break rooms, ping-pong tables, or video games to provide relief from stress. The cafeteria is a small room where a couple of sweet ladies prepare food that's reminiscent of the kind you would get in an elementary-school lunchroom. There are no stock options for technicians. And yet, the employee turnover rate is less than 5 per cent per year. The cooperation between employees is high and the team performance is extraordinary, though the work is no less difficult than rocket science,' wrote Charles Fishman, an award-winning investigative and magazine journalist, about the General Electric plant in Durham, North Carolina. GE Durham builds some of the world's most powerful jet engines. However, the plant's real power lies in the lessons that it offers on social capital, and how the company manages to nurture horizontal ties helping it to manage day-to-day affairs.

'GE Durham has more than 170 employees but just one boss: the plant manager.' Fishman continues, 'Which means that on a day-to-day basis, the people who work here have no boss. They essentially cooperate and run the show themselves. The jet engines are produced by nine teams of people and teams that are given just one basic directive: the day that their next engine must be loaded onto a truck. All other decisions—who does what work; how to balance training, vacations, overtime against workflow; how to make the manufacturing process more efficient; how to handle teammates who slack off—all of that stays within the team. Yet, people who work at this plant try to make perfect jet engines. And they come close. On average, one quarter of the engines that GE Durham sends to Boeing have just a single defect—something cosmetic, such as a cable not lined up right, or a scratch on a fan case. The other three quarters are, in fact, perfect.'

Getting individuals to collaborate with each other even when they do not have the lure of incentives or the fear of punishments is definitely not an easy task, which is exactly the reason why we are impressed when we hear stories like that of GE Durham. However, not too long ago, the popular idea was that we have an abstract and innate tendency to organize and cooperate with each other towards common goals. But soon, we found that though it is easy to subscribe to this grand optimism, it is still a tight rope walk; of motivating people to refrain from individually profitable actions for the sake of common good.

Mancur Olson in his book, *Logic of Collective Action*, writes about this: 'If the members of some group have a common interest, and if they would all be better off if that objective were achieved, it has been thought to follow logically that the individuals in that group would, if they were rational and self-interested, act to achieve that objective.' Then he went on to challenge this presumption that the possibility of a benefit for a group would be sufficient to generate collective action to achieve that benefit. In the most frequently quoted passage of his book, he argued that unless the number of individuals was quite small or unless there was coercion or some other special device to make individuals act in their common interest, rational self-interested individuals would not act to achieve their common or group interests.

> Unless there is coercion or incentive, people do not automatically cooperate even when they have a common interest.

Researchers Alberto Alesina and Joan Esteban suggest that heterogeneity could be a great hurdle to individuals voluntarily cooperating in a group. This could be true from three angles. First, heterogeneity in a group can generate distinct group identities between members, increasing perceived inequalities which affect cooperation. Second, individuals might simply dislike working with others outside their group, thus making cooperation less likely in heterogeneous communities. Third, heterogeneous communities would find it hard to agree on the characteristics of the common goal versus their individual goals and would be therefore less likely to cooperate in its provision. Therefore, homogeneous communities might be better at solving collective action problems because all members had similar tastes and could get on to easier agreements on points of discontent. However, we know that this is not as easy as it sounds, because any randomly chosen groups across organizations tend to be more heterogeneous than homogeneous. But there is good news. Open Source leadership organizations have consistently demonstrated that it is possible to create homogeneity even in the most diverse groups. (At the same time, there is a difference in the way Open Source leadership views the concept of homogeneity itself. This is brought out through the 'melting pot' and 'salad bowl' model in Chapter 7.)

The first step towards homogeneity is thinking about homogeneity from the first organizational step onwards. Ashish Nehra knows how his captain worked on this. 'Sourav went out of his way to make sure that we were creating a team where everyone is comfortable with everyone else. The team already had Rahul Dravid, Sachin Tendulkar, V.V.S. Laxman and Anil Kumble, seniors in the team and close friends, since they had been playing together for long. So, Sourav focused on building the rest of the team with those players who would not only gel with the seniors but also with each other, with no baggage of seniority or egos. He actively campaigned and supported the younger lot like Yuvraj Singh, Harbhajan Singh, Virender Sehwag, Zaheer Khan and Mohammed Kaif. We could together build a good team because Sourav created a great atmosphere where we could all play and have fun together. More than just players, we were all good buddies: juniors, seniors, the captain and the coach.

'Further, Sourav also reiterated continuously that our journey was not limited to a few years, but would last a lifetime. We would have to continue seeing each other, in various capacities, and have to continue working together, even after our cricketing careers were over. That helped putting things into perspective. Any short-term individual opportunistic interests were mitigated. People knew that they were in this for a long haul. So we all came together, supported each other and helped each other succeed.'

A sure-fire way of ensuring homogeneity, which in turn ensures voluntary cooperation, is by bringing together people who have interests in each other beyond just professional pursuits. In the case of Ganguly, he made sure that his team comprised a group of young chaps who were fired with enthusiasm, who understood and supported each other. However, this was possible, without too much difficulty, primarily because professional cricketing is a small circuit, where people get to know each other and get to judge each other easily. Whether they like it or not, they end up meeting each other and playing with and against each other several times a year during domestic and other matches. Ganguly's task was again made easier, since the national team comprised just a handful of individuals, who were selected with a longer stint in mind.

However, larger organizations would not have this advantage. Especially in cases like Art of Living, which boasts of a presence across the globe and tens of thousands of new members every year.

Vikram Hazra, a full-time volunteer at Art of Living is probably the best example for why ensuring homogeneity by relying on a few external attributes is a very difficult proposition. Vikram is the lead coordinator and teacher for the corporate programmes of Art of Living. He comes from a media background, where he has been a producer and a journalist. An initial glance reveals nothing that connects him with the several other volunteers around—some housewives, some teachers, some from corporate backgrounds, while many others are retirees. However, Vikram claims that there is a connect, something which is hardly noticed. Vikram explains: 'To an outsider there is nothing much that binds me to someone like Swamy Pragyapath or for that matter to anyone else around. We come from diverse places and environments. Yet, at some point of time we have all thought about a larger sense of belongingness to our world. All Art of Living people are bound by a sense of responsibility, outside what one considers one's purview, to this world. We feel that we have a greater sense of ownership and from there we derive an expanded sense of belongingness. You cannot see it, but you can feel it. That is what connects me to all the others over here.

'We have no control over who volunteers to join Art of Living,' Vikram continues, 'and we cannot prevent someone, even if we feel that he does not fit in. That is a constraint in trying to build a homogeneous community. But at the same time we know that, though this person may not resemble most others in the community, he will still fit in, if he is moved by this sense of responsibility and this cause. Else, he himself would prefer to go out after some time. So, we do not decide who fits in, the person himself decides.'

> Step one to break horizontal barriers: To make people aware that they are in it for a long haul and not for a short term. This will minimize short-term, self-interest-motivated defections.

Homogeneity in a community helps immensely in solving many of the collaboration problems—in discouraging opportunistic behaviour and promoting cooperation—even in the absence of coercion or any physical incentives. However, not all groups are as blessed as the Indian cricket team, where Sourav Ganguly could ensure homogeneity from the very start or like Art of Living, where volunteers buy into a mighty vision. Most organizations come with baggage, and most others collect their baggage as they go along. Here people would increasingly draw away from each other as they go through the frictions of their everyday lives. Even if they started out homogeneous, these frictions would ensure that they are on their way to heterogeneity, killing cooperation and collective action in the process.

Open Source Leaders deploy a couple of surprisingly simple techniques to fight this daily wear and tear in homogeneity—coffee table conversations and long lunch breaks. In most companies, these are considered a waste of productive employee time. However, open leaders understand that, if properly utilized and channelized, these typical time wasters can be used to enhance cooperation and collaboration between people.

Zappos.com, an online apparel and footwear company ranked among the 'Fortune 100 Best Companies to Work For' in 2009, is almost a legend of sorts for the unique culture that it promotes, where social capital is given importance over everything, even over the bottom line of the company. Tony Hsieh, the CEO of Zappos.com, originally got involved with the company as an advisor and investor in 1999, a couple of months after the company was formed. Eventually, Tony ended up joining the company full time, because he found it the most interesting and promising out of all the companies that he had ever been involved with.

'Zappos is nothing like a traditional company. It is informal, almost like a family. We have worked hard on getting to this environment. We encourage our people to hang out even outside the office through dinner, drinks and parties. We encourage our managers, especially during their orientation, to spend 10 to 20 per cent of their time outside the office with their employees, whether it is a picnic, or hiking or whatever. They are constantly hanging around with each other.

'Some of them are sceptical during the orientation programme; hence we refer them to our other managers who have done this earlier. We ask our managers regularly through surveys and during meetings on how much more efficient their teams are because there is more trust and personal interaction between their people. The answers range between 20 to 100 per cent. In the worst case scenario, you break even if you spend 10 to 20 per cent of your time outside the office. Hanging around is not just fun, but also makes business sense,' says Tony.

'While you are on the field you are focused. You are working on something, you are improving your game, and so you might not get time to talk to your teammates at all. But off the field you have dinners and other functions. Prior to Sourav, these were seen as typical time wasters—something that would take away the focus of players. But during Sourav's time we started enjoying our dinners, team official functions and sponsors' functions. Those were seen as time to get to know the different side of cricketers. We also quickly learnt that these were not just vain chit-chat times, but a productive time for preparing for the game. I realized you also learnt a lot during dinners—by watching other good cricketers, how they prepared for the game and how they moved around when they were in public,' explains Ashish Nehra.

Tony also has a similar reasoning on why such informal gatherings help business. He says, 'The top line and bottom line are not our competitive advantages. Our competitive advantage is this open culture. There are higher levels of efficiency because there is more transparent communication and more trust between the members. We do favours for each other, personal ones, because we are friends more than co-workers. It is more fun when you also get to work with your friends than with co-workers whom you see just on a professional basis. There are also higher levels of loyalty to the organization, and hence lower levels of attrition. For most of them, this is where their friends are. If they were to leave, they would not only cease to be a part of the company, but would also be leaving their friends. They would not get a chance to meet up with them on a daily basis.'

Step two to break horizontal barriers: Daily frictions can cause wear and tear in the team homogeneity. Build informal occasions to oil and smoothen these out.

In a 1985 paper, psychologist Dennis Fox, after having reviewed several sets of experimental data, argued that voluntary cooperative behaviour tends to be more common and entrenched in smaller groups compared to larger ones. Many believe that this better efficiency in smaller groups might have to do with our evolution as hunter-gatherer communities, when we operated out of a home base and utilized considerable cooperation and communication. Another psychologist, Robin Dunbar, in his writings, suggested that human beings have a real limitation in that they are actually equipped only to handle smaller groups. According to his findings, we would require bigger brains if we have to handle living in big groups, to keep track of all the complex relationships needed to live in relative peaceful cooperation. But in smaller groups, people can afford to have a genuine social relationship, the kind of relationship where we know who they are and how they relate to us. However, once these groups exceed a certain size (in the absence of bigger brains, as Ram Raghavan suggests), hierarchical structure becomes a necessity—to enforce the rules of cooperation and to deal with offenders. Still larger groups demand stricter rule enforcements, which involve more violence or threats of violence.

The size of the group also has an implication on the way we conduct ourselves in organizations. It is easier to be an offender or to defect when group sizes are large, since one can go unnoticed. This is another reason why classical Taylorism, formulated to address the problems of large manufacturing-style set-ups (often involving thousands or even tens of thousands) insisted on highly centralized, stringent rules-driven workplaces. However, Open Source leadership realizes the importance of smaller groups compared to larger ones, and hence operates in such ways as to leverage this.

'The volunteer strength of Art of Living is enormous. It is easy for any person to be lost in this vast ocean—of not only people, but also space and distances. Quite early, we came to grip with this reality. People would come in large numbers, but they would soon lose their enthusiasm because they were not visible, no matter how hard they tried. Hence, we always make it a point to keep our teams as small as possible. Even in larger projects, we insist on smaller groups—each one around twenty members or so. The biggest advantage of smaller groups is the fact that everyone knows everyone else. Everything works on voluntary cooperation. It is almost like a pot-pourri of several families,' explains Vikram.

When Tony Hsieh took over Zappos, it was just over a million-dollar company. Now it has grown to about a billion dollars, and continues to grow at a rapid pace. Tony says they are still able to keep up the distinctive culture by focusing on maintaining the feel of a small company.

'It is impossible to know every employee as the company grows bigger. Everyone wears a name badge and the location. When you log in to the back-end system, every day there is a game where you see a random face and you are trying to guess the name of the person. We do things like that. Yet, there are limitations. Hence, we focus on different departments and different teams. We make sure that people are in small enough teams where they cannot hide. We build close-knit communities inside these teams, each of which have around ten members, by encouraging them to hang around together, be it inside the office or outside,' Tony says.

Step three to break horizontal barriers: Keep each group small. Break down larger groups into smaller subgroups.

Dr Richard Ian Charlesworth, popularly known as Ric Charlesworth has seen both sides of the game—that of a player and that of a coach. He represented the Australian hockey team in five Olympic games, two of which he captained, and was part of the World Cup winning team in 1986. For more than a decade, he was regarded as the world's best hockey player. After his playing career ended, he went on to be the head coach for the Australian women's hockey team 'Hockeyroos', during which time they conquered almost all the known hockey challenges across the world, including the Champion's Trophy, the World Cup, Olympics and the Commonwealth Games.

However, Ric Charlesworth is not your traditional coach. He has almost been a revolutionary of sorts in his approach while building winning teams. He developed a strategy, which he refers to as a 'Leaderful Team', where every player is developed to recognize their own and others' strengths and limitations, and prepared technically and psychologically, to step up to lead, or step back and support as needed. In short, the Leaderful Team approach aimed at maximizing the contribution of every team member in a way never before attempted in sport.

'In our Leaderful Team, Hockeyroos, everyone who had something to contribute was provided with the opportunity to do so,' explained Ric. 'In a large group, it is difficult for people to contribute and be seen. But if you break the team down into smaller groups, people in each group can take initiatives. So, we had this group of almost thirty people, plus the support staff of about ten or fifteen, which made a fairly large team size. We formed a range of committees, or if you like to call them, small groups, within the team. Each committee was responsible for particular parts of our game—say one group was responsible for training, one was responsible for social environment, one was responsible for looking at other sports to learn things from them, while one was responsible for scouting the other teams. Each one of these committees had leaders who were expected to work towards their goal.

'In a larger group, people could have engaged in social loafing. While the leader and a few people worked, this majority felt not so engaged, not so curious, not so interested and not so willing to put forward their ideas. So you did not get from them what they had to offer. But when we built smaller committees, people were more willing to contribute. Suddenly, the team was brimming with leaders. Instead of one leader, who took up all responsibilities, got paid more, and got more media attention, now we had a bunch of people, all owning up responsibilities and taking leadership. They understood that there was no leadership hierarchy, and hence concentrated all their efforts towards playing better. The team was truly "leaderful".

'In Hockeyroos, we constantly strived to increase the number of leaders in the team. We had as many as six or eight leaders at some point of time. No one held the "only one leader" mantle. We shared the load evenly and even rotated the positions between people. No one is excluded from holding a responsibility. There was less infighting and less politics in the group because people were no longer trying to become the captain. Holding the position of a captain was no longer an exhausting proposition loaded with duties, but a pleasurable one,' suggests Ric.

> Step four to break horizontal barriers: Develop 'leaderful' teams, where leaders are nurtured to take up more accountabilities in each of the smaller teams.

Robert Putnam writes about another solution, drawn from the wisdom of small group structures, for improving the cooperation between individuals in an organization. He calls this a honeycomb structure, where the organization offers its people many opportunities to interact at deeper levels. A honeycomb structure is essentially a conglomeration of several small groups, within an organization, not necessarily connected with the core business of the company, but which helps its people to connect with each other and develop trust in each other. These smaller groups have low entry barriers—anyone who is interested can associate as well as contribute. It is easy to enter and it is easy to leave.

Putnam suggests that when individuals are allowed to interact and communicate beyond their normal routine professional commitments, cooperation improves. 'The intense tie is not to an ideology but in the emotional commitment to others in their small group. Most of these people are seeking a profession, whereby they can earn their bread, but they are also seeking friends. These small groups allow them to spend time together, away from professional commitments, and getting to know and trust each other—be it by playing a part in a sports club, cooperatives, mutual aid societies, cultural associations or voluntary unions—they become your closest friends.'

A good place to get a feel of these honeycomb structures is from GE Durham, where in addition to the core job of building engines, everyone serves on one of several work councils that cut across team lines. Fishman reports that some of these councils handle HR issues, supplier problems, engineering challenges, computer systems, discipline, and rewards. People also get together in smaller groups for organizing frequent training sessions—from sessions on how to give and receive feedback to advanced classes on cost accounting—all of which help people break down those barriers that they erected during their work in their closed walls of professional commitments.

These smaller groups, incidentally, also help people in buying into, empathizing with and understanding some of the larger values of the organization. For example, during their time in the smaller work councils, GE Durham people learn the ropes of 'decision making through consensus', one of the founding principles here. Their learning grows from smaller consensus among smaller groups of people on smaller issues like where to go for lunch or whom to hire, towards larger ones with greater implications like how to organize a production line and how to run a factory. They learn how to drive smaller and bigger changes, and how to live with ideas that they might not necessarily agree with.

Step five to break horizontal barriers: Build smaller honeycomb structures with low entry barriers, beyond normal routine professional commitments, where people can connect with each other and develop trust in each other.

Honeycomb structures, such as the ones in GE Durham, help in building a collaborative environment by simulating almost real-life situations, but with considerably lesser amount of risk for the organization, since these are not directly connected with the core business. There is yet another way—exposure to complex problems—in fact almost diametrically opposite to honeycomb structures, that Open Source Leaders engage to build cooperation. These complex problems are several times more complicated than any normal task that an individual would handle in the group. They require more experience than any single person can possess. The knowledge relevant to these kinds of problems is often distributed among several people who have different perspectives and background knowledge. Hence, for a solution, people are forced to tap into the skills and potential of others around them—enabling the creation of newer networks, increased trust and shared understanding in the process.

The reward for facilitating complex problems does not stop there. They also provide the foundation for social creativity—a term coined by Gerhard Fischer from the University of Colorado to refer to creativity arising from activities that take place in a social context in which interaction with other people and the artefacts that embody collective knowledge are essential contributors. Bringing together different points of view and trying to create a shared understanding among all contributors can lead to new ideas that would not have been created in normal team situations. His analysis of creative people has demonstrated that most scientific and artistic innovations emerge from joint thinking, passionate conversations, and shared struggles among different people, emphasizing the importance of the social dimension of creativity.

Mired in controversies and low performances, the most complex problem that the Indian cricket team had to solve was winning their games. Joseph Hoover, a veteran sports journalist says about this, 'It was not that the team did not want to win, but somehow something was not clicking. We were just not able to hold our fort together. Then there was this talk of the division in the team—South boys, Mumbai boys, Delhi boys, etc. When Sourav got the captaincy he declared that he would do everything in his might to facilitate the team. Firstly, he created a sense of security among team members and transparency in selection. In return, he asked them to go out, play their best and win the games. Slowly but steadily, they started realizing the seriousness of the task. They realized that it is not only about individual goals, or landmarks, but also about aligning these goals to bigger team goals. It is not just that I perform well, but my team should also perform well. Players slowly started backing each other up. Everybody started motivating each other, everyone started to take time out to analyse each other, to push each other up to the next level of performance. And as they started gelling together in the context of winning, they found their rhythm somewhere around 2002, about two years after Ganguly took over as the captain. They started winning games—the One-Day series against Zimbabwe, against the West Indies, the NatWest series in England, the ICC Champions Trophy in Sri Lanka and to the finals of the World Cup 2003.'

Step six to break horizontal barriers: Expose the team to complex problems, where they are forced to draw upon the strengths and skills of everyone for a solution.

In the modern world, where organizations swear by the latest management practices—most of which consider the relationship between the organization and its people as contractual—Open Source leadership stands apart. These organizations still believe in the old world wisdom that if people are allowed not only to work together but also to have fun together, they would work more smoothly and collaborate more easily. Some of these organizations have opted to completely rely on informal collaboration mechanisms, while most of them mix and match— formal management practices along with informal collaboration mechanisms. And they are finding that this new arrangement is working well. It is helping them bring down their transaction costs—the cost of all the information processing and monitoring necessary to coordinate the work of people. More importantly, it is helping them stay true to what they are, to stay far away from the tyranny of an all-powerful top management, often representative of an excessively rigid and unresponsive system.

4

Break Glass in Case of Emergency
Open Source Leadership Eliminates All
Glass Ceilings to Create a Transparent and
Meritocratic Workplace

In this section:
- Understanding a ceiling that looks like glass but is as tough as steel
- Why Open Source leadership is not played like the 'dictator game'
- How Open Source leadership uses a weapon of 'voice' to weed out the frustrations expressed near water coolers, smoking zones and washrooms
- How Open Source leadership not only gives people their 'voice' but also teaches them to scream

Understanding a ceiling that looks like glass but is as tough as steel

Patrick Kiger, a freelance writer, once wrote the story of an employee from W.L. Gore—one of the largest privately held companies in the USA—who once found herself in a strange dilemma. She had to attend an outside conference and the hosts expected her to have a job title. However, this was something which she along with all the other people at her company were never provided with. At Gore, they believed that such distinctions erected a 'glass ceiling'—a term initially used by researchers to indicate invisible barriers that impeded the career advancement of women. Since then the term has almost become generic, referring to all those situations where the advancement of a competent person is curtailed because of some form of biased perception.

71

Glass barriers are unofficial, unwritten and invisible, but they are definitely present in every organization.

Many of the social psychologists attribute the existence of the glass ceilings to the manner in which human beings process information (the same reflections can be seen in Chapter 1, Ram Raghavan's argument of the human brain operating at a miniscule 100 hertz and in Chapter 3, Robin Dunbar's research about human beings equipped to handle only smaller groups). In order to make sense of a complex social environment, we group individuals into categories and associate them with specific attributes. Stereotyping is typically the result. This, in and of itself, is not necessarily an inappropriate means of processing information, because it allows an individual to quickly interpret stimuli and make a response. However, in an organizational context, this stereotyping could mean someone underestimating the potential of an individual altogether. It could reflect unrecognized biases about such an individual's attributes, abilities, commitment and flexibility within the workplace resulting in serious consequences on performance evaluations, assignments and growth. Designations, as Bill Gore, the founder of W.L. Gore suspected, could add to this corporate stereotyping pretty well. For example, it is easy to presume that the potential of an accounting clerk is much less than that of a manager, an assumption based on the position that they are holding, but the reality could be completely different. According to Gore, designations stifled freedom, communication and creativity.

However, in the case of our employee who was desperately in need of a designation, Bill Gore is said to have offered a quick suggestion—to call herself 'supreme commander'. The employee reportedly liked it so much that she had business cards printed with that inscription. The first one was handed over to Bill Gore himself.

Corporate stereotyping and in turn glass ceilings arise from a perception problem, which is slightly different from that of the trust problem that we saw in the previous chapter. While over there, the challenge was the trust of the people in their leader, here it is the trust of the leader in his people. Many stereotypes spring up when a leader doubts the ability of his people in shouldering responsibilities—responsibilities that are anything more than the typical ones that they routinely handle. Somehow, here the assumption is that people do not have the potential to handle greater responsibilities, and hence cannot be trusted. The only way they could be convinced to let their people take up bigger responsibilities is by allowing them to put more controls in place. They would trust these controls more than their people.

Management thinker Rob Lebow suggests that traditional closed organizations keep people as well as their performances under check by imposing controls through obvious as well as not so obvious mechanisms like hierarchical structures, direct and indirect supervision, management quotas and even through stereotyping methods like designations. Even namesake empowerment is usually responsibility without any authority. Authority always rests with the leader, because that gives him the security of his control over his people.

However, Open Source leadership handles things differently. It is based on the understanding that every person can do his best, want to do his best and even need to do his best, but none of these is possible if he is surrounded by barriers that are forcing him to play below his potential. The practitioners understand that the main issue is not one of control resting with the leader, but that of sincerely helping every individual to contribute his best, even if that results in an insecure leader. Open Source leadership moves the focus away from a leader's emotions to those of his people.

ICICI Bank is probably one of the few organizations, even worldwide, where most of the senior leadership positions have historically been adorned by women, including the current managing director and CEO Chanda Kochhar. A surprising fact, considering that corporate stereotyping is the most rampant in the gender arena. In fact, the term glass ceiling, as we saw earlier, has its origins in the discriminatory behaviour towards women, where they often faced obstacles in obtaining and securing the most powerful, prestigious and highest-grossing jobs in the workforce. While on the one hand these glass ceilings made them feel unworthy of high-ranking positions, on the other they continuously made them feel underestimated.

N. Vaghul, who was one of India's youngest chairmen of a nationalized bank in India and who retired as the chairman of ICICI Bank, after adorning that position for close to twenty-four years, is probably the best person to comment about this prominence of women at ICICI Bank. He attributes this phenomenon to the fact that the bank always had the fewest of barriers when it came to the professional growth of women. At the same time, he is quick to assert that this is not a result of any preferential treatment doled out to them. The rules are clear, you rise to your position not because of your gender, but because you are talented. Even during the initial stages, ICICI Bank took special care to remain gender neutral, which meant that whenever they recruited, they did not care whether it was a man or a woman. They only cared about the competency and nothing else. This ensured larger representation of women in the system, which in turn ensured the rise of a large number of managers and general managers who were women. Vaghul says it was not easy being neutral, since in any male-dominated society it was easy to be accused of being pro-woman for being neutral.

Chanda Kochhar says that she learnt this lesson—to be neutral to everything else other than sheer performance—very early in her career from her predecessors including Vaghul. According to her, most people do not require a preferential treatment or special privileges to rise to their true potential. All that they would require is equality. ICICI Bank makes sure that they practise this value, not only inside, but also in other arenas that they have control over. For example, the bank has set up self-help groups in the rural villages, each of them comprising twenty people. Women who have until then been socially excluded and living on the fringes, emerge the most proactive to change and progress, as they are exposed to new opportunities. 'They are now the driving forces in many of these villages,' Chanda comments.

Anindya Banerjee, a young man from Kolkata, is a general manager and the executive assistant to K. V. Kamat, the chairman of ICICI Bank. Sitting in their plush conference room in Bandra–Kurla Complex, Mumbai, he suggests that he himself is good proof of how people can grow, if an organization promoted a truly glass ceiling-free environment. Though Anindya operated from a zonal office in distant Kolkata, his work was noticed up to the level of the managing director, primarily because the bank promoted an environment where smaller offices were given equal footage alongside the headquarters, quite unlike larger organizations. Smaller offices formed a vital and vibrant link in cross-pollination of talent, ideas and power and were not discriminated against. 'There are no glass barriers between the people in the headquarters and those from the branch offices. You could be anywhere in the system, but if you are doing good work you would get noticed. It is clearly the talent and results that matter, not the space you operate out of,' comments Anindya.

Formidable potential from people at the fringe level could be unleashed in organizations, if glass ceilings, consisting of inherent biases towards them, could be weeded out. A leader cannot expect his people to do their best if they continue to have policies and beliefs based on presumptions that discriminate. You just cannot discriminate people and at the same time empower them. It just would not work.

Step one to break glass ceilings: Most people do not require any preferential treatment, but just equality to be more productive. So, be neutral to everything but performance.

Why Open Source leadership is not played like the 'dictator game'

In traditional closed organizations, people are treaded upon ruthlessly to make way for the organizational bottom line. Leaders take advantage of their followers by exploiting their potential as if it is a dictator game—a simple model in behavioural economics devised to give a peek into the human behaviour. In the dictator game, the first player, 'the proposer', determines an allocation of some endowment. The second player, 'the responder', simply receives what the proposer determines or what is remaining. The responder's role in the game is entirely passive, since he has no strategic input into the outcome of the game. In fact, many economists do not even consider this formally as a game at all, because they argue that to be called a game, every player's outcome must depend on the actions of at least some others. In a dictator game, the proposer's outcome does not depend on anyone else's action, while the responder's outcome depends completely on the mercy of the proposer. Traditional closed organizations play the dictator game every day, where the talents, careers, opportunities and growth of the majority of individuals depend on one or a few individuals. These few individuals dictate how the game has to be played; they frame the rules and the barriers and they play favourites, helping those whom they prefer and blocking whom they dislike. The majority remain as passive responders—either hanging on or tearing their hair in dissatisfaction.

'In Biocon there is no barrier to individual growth. The only barrier between you and your growth is yourself. Nothing else,' comments Susan Kumar, the executive secretary to Kiran Mazumdar Shaw, the chairperson, referred to as 'India's Mother of Invention' by the *New York Times*. Founded in 1978, with a paltry investment of US$500, currently Biocon is one of the largest biotechnology companies in the world, listed among the 'Best under a Billion' by *Forbes*. Susan says that it is this meritocratic culture, where barriers are minimized so that people could be made directly responsible for their growth, that is the real secret behind the growth of her company. She explains this through a nice analogy: Biocon is not a huge single-trunk coconut tree, but a banyan tree, held together with branches from various sources. The main trunk that carries the vision of Biocon is important, but the branches, which are the individuals, their hopes and aspirations, are equally important. 'People are not forced to give up on their individual goals here, but are encouraged and are actively pushed to move towards what they really want. For us, responsible growth means responsibility towards every individual working here. And as they move forward, Biocon moves forward.'

Murli Krishnan has been working in Biocon since 1981. He is one of their oldest employees, from the time the company operated out of a garage, and is currently the president of Group Finance. Murli says his family always wanted him to join one of the public sector banks. Interestingly, one of his uncles even went ahead and arranged an interview for him with one of the banks. Murli was confident that he could get selected, because he had the requisite knowledge and skill. However, he was doubtful whether this was the place where he would like to spend the rest of his life. He never wanted to be one of the thousands of employees sitting at their desk, waiting for the day to end or the next promotion to come by. Murli decided to pass the opportunity. Of course, his family was upset with this decision, but Murli stood firm.

Instead, Murli started with Biocon as a part-time help to the auditor, where he rode down to work every day on his small motorcycle. After about six months or so, noticing the good work, Kiran asked him whether he would be interested in a full-time assignment. Murli recalls that Biocon was small at that point of time, by any stretch of imagination. 'It could never be compared to the size of any public sector bank, nor could I compare it to the security that the bank job offered me. To add to my confusion, I knew if I took up a full-time assignment, I would not have time to complete my chartered accountancy course. Yet, I decided to take it up. Because I knew intuitively that this was the place. It was small, but it accommodated my aspirations. It was empathetic to my dreams. It did not stand in the way of my personal dreams. The decision was easy.'

Dr Arun Chandavarkar, a chemical engineer from the MIT and chief operating officer at Biocon, reflects on the same thought that Murli Krishnan has planted. 'I could have had a career in the US, since I am reasonably westernized and had lived there for six years. It was not a deep sense of patriotism either, since the quality of life, in terms of conveniences could not be compared, especially twenty years back. Interestingly, I even had an offer from Unilever. The decision could have been easy. Because when Kiran made me an offer to join Biocon, it was almost a non-entity. Salaries again were not comparable. Yet, I knew that Biocon would do justice to my career. An open culture would mean I could get on to the fast lane easier. I could grow as Biocon grew.'

Open Source leadership, like Susan Kumar described, is all about individual aspirations woven together to a greater vision. It is not played like a dictator game, where nothing matters except for the larger organizational vision or the motives of a few individual leaders. In Open Source leadership people like Murli Krishnan and Arun Chandavarkar find a safe refuge. They do not have to sacrifice their personal goals at the altar of their organizational mission.

> Step two to break glass ceilings: It is not only about organizational goals, but also about individual aspirations.

At the same time, Open Source leadership has to ensure that this openness towards individual aspirations is not exploited by a few selfish individuals who are typically job hoppers—cooling their heels during their search for the next best destination. It takes just a few individuals to spoil the game, to distort it in unexpected ways to their advantage. Breaking glass barriers is also about selecting the right people, and then helping them with their dreams.

Susan Kumar comes up with another analogy: 'Bees are attracted to honey. If you attract the right kind of people, you would continue to grow responsibly to the organization as well as to its individuals. If you take in the wrong people, you cannot presume that they would transform, even if you put in efforts.

'More than the right qualifications, to survive in this kind of an open atmosphere, you should have the right mindset. Fine-tuning is the value addition that Biocon creates. It is like the icing on the cake. The cake itself is very tasty, the icing just adds to the presentation.'

Incidentally, Patrick Kiger writes the same thing about W.L. Gore. He writes that Gore's recruiters spend months, sometimes years filling up job vacancies, because it is not easy to find people who not only have the right business skills, but also are temperamentally and intellectually suited for the unorthodox environment. It is not a company for everyone because it takes a special kind of person to be effective in a special kind of environment.

A veteran sales executive of W.L. Gore, John Cusick had this to say in an article, 'Success at Gore has little to do with a classical education; many of Gore's top associates never finished college. It is about a certain fit, a confluence with the culture. In sales there is special anxiety in hiring, since many candidates come from traditional corporate bureaucracies, where sales is often treated as a singular pursuit, driven by money and rooted in individual achievement. Those people would probably bring in a lot of sales for the company, but they would not be happy here because our company is different.'

Zappos pays a little extra attention making sure that only the right candidates get in to the system, primarily because over and above maintaining their unique culture, they also have the tough task of keeping people in a profile that is otherwise perceived as boring—a call centre. Max Chafkin writes in Inc.com that Zappos surmounts this challenge by creating wildly different expectations from most companies. For example, prospective hires must pass an hour-long 'culture interview' before being handed over to whichever department they are applying to. Questions include, 'On a scale of one to ten, how weird are you?' and 'Who is your favourite superhero, and why?' etc. If there is a disagreement between HR and the department doing the hiring, Hsieh personally interviews the candidate, where he gets him to a social situation to see whether they can connect emotionally, before making the final call.

However, the most important 'culture fit test' in Zappos comes after the candidate has been selected, according to Tony. 'After an employee has come in and has been trained, we offer him $2000 to quit—a substantial sum for a call centre trainee. The idea is to weed out anyone with doubts about whether Zappos is really for him. We make sure that we are left with a set of people who are absolutely passionate about their job as well as to the culture.'

Step three to break glass ceilings: If you attract the right kind of people, it would become easier for you to break glass ceilings. Else, the open system will get exploited.

How Open Source leadership uses a weapon of 'voice' to weed out the frustrations expressed near water coolers, smoking zones and washrooms

Albert Hirschman, an influential economist, suggested that in a typical organizational atmosphere, people can resort to two options when they face dissatisfaction. They can either choose to exit, that is, leave the relationship, or voice out—attempt to change the relationship from within through complaints, grievances or proposals of change. Employees can choose to quit their unpleasant job, or express their concerns in an effort to improve the situation.

The options—exit and voice—interact in unique and sometimes unexpected ways in organizations. If people are provided with greater freedom and greater opportunities for feedback and criticism, they would use little of the exit option. Conversely, stifling of dissent would lead to increased pressure for members of the organization to use their only other means available to express discontent—departure. The general principle, therefore, is that greater the availability of voice, the less likely exit would be used.

Reliance on Hirschman's strategy of voice is a way in which Open Source leadership creates a special environment that differentiates themselves from others. Susan Kumar reflects, 'In most organizations, secretaries are put in their place. They are clearly made to feel like secretaries, as order takers. Interestingly, this restriction to the role of an order taker is not specific to secretaries alone. It is a universal phenomenon, where at every level everyone gets orders from a higher level. No orders are challenged; no questions are asked or expected. If anyone stands up, he becomes the odd one out. At the same time, from these order takers, there is no great loyalty or attachment—to their seniors or to the role. It is like a contract, where people are waiting to move on.'

However, Susan says that Biocon is at the other end of the spectrum, where everyone can voice his opinions not just about his immediate tasks, but also about anything that concerns him in the organization. She continues in a philosophical tone, 'Opinions are almost like my alter ego. Where my opinions count, I count. Where I am heard, I am respected. If some say that I am important to them, but do not give ears to my concerns, it just means that they are being hypocritical. And if someone says that there are no barriers to my growth, but is not willing to listen, I am just being exploited to meet somebody else's vested interests.'

Voicing out can help in dealing with individual frustrations inside an organizational system. Because as people become nothing more than order takers, they increasingly get the feeling that most decisions that concern them as well as their organization are outside their control. Things are pre-decided and all that they can do is be satisfied with the role of passive spectators.

Susan Kumar says, 'Many a time, in organizations, people have this lingering feeling that the outcome could have been much better if they were allowed to contribute. Several people in the fringe might have great ideas that could add much value to the organization, but would never express it, unless they are very bold, because previous experiences have told them that there are little chances that anyone would pay attention to them. In fact, chances are that they would be scoffed at. Hence, the best strategy for any employee is to just remain silent. Just do the task allotted to him and get out when the day is over. However, this silence has a negative side—frustration. Every employee in such a system would be frustrated. Such employees keep complaining all the time—to themselves and to their close groups of friends. Near the water coolers, smoking zones or washrooms, they are complaining all the time about issues that they feel are not justified inside the organization.

'Apart from wasting productive time, these frustrations and constant whining also lead to a lot of pent-up negative energy inside the system. People continue working for lack of options. The minute they have some, they are more than happy to go out. So, in a way, people are constantly working towards failing the system instead of making it succeed. But systems like Biocon are different because here people are part of the system. The minute people are really a part, they do not have an option but to help it succeed. Because the system's success then becomes "my" success.' Susan opens up.

This is easier said than done. People who are used to traditional closed organizations (which most of us are) would not just stand up and speak out, if they are put in to an Open Source leadership environment one fine day. Their previous experiences have taught them that voicing out is a triple-edged weapon—if it is against your boss's opinion you are immediately in his bad book; if it fails, you get blamed for it; and if it succeeds, your boss gets the credit and you get none. Therefore, as Susan described, for anyone with a little sense, the best strategy is to be silent. Hirschman suggests that in such an organization, the exit itself would happen in one of two ways. The first kind of exit is the physical exit where a person decides to quit and go out of the system. In the second kind, the exit is not physical but mental or emotional. For example, if people are not in a physical condition to exit, probably because they have lesser choices or have a family to support, they would choose to emotionally shut down. They would be neither loyal nor would they be willing to voice their dissatisfaction. The consequences of this exit can sometimes be more hazardous compared to the simple physical exit because unsatisfied people continue to be a part of the system, working against it rather than for it. This is in line with the work of Wilfred Bion at the Tavistock Clinic in London on group psychology, where he suggested that many members in traditional closed organizations unconsciously fight with or flee from leadership rather than join in productive activity.

Open Source leadership realizes that building the true voices of the people inside their organizations is a tough process. Because people who are used to the conventional way of doing things would choose to go through the path of least resistance—where they choose not to voice out—even in an open environment. But at the same time, if people continue being in such a frame of mind, where they are shut down physically and emotionally, there would not be any Open Source leadership, since voice happens to be one of the pillars.

A good first step to enable people give up their path of least resistance is opening unto them information which was previously inaccessible. Information is one of the important weapons which a leader uses to build his influence. Access to it is the key in deciding where the influence is tipped towards. It helps a leader to build his power, because he owns something which others don't; it helps him wield his power inside the organization, because he can assess situations in ways that fit into his agenda and drive decisions in ways useful to him. It is also a zero-sum game. It not only makes the leader more powerful, but also makes others weak and dependent. Without relevant information, even if people would like to be involved in decision making, they would not be. If they muster the courage to do so, the probabilities are high that it might not fit into the context and hence could appear silly.

Sandeep Bhargava, CEO of Studio18 comments, 'Leaders normally safeguard information because of their vested interests. If a leader has a vested interest in a certain outcome, he would always make it a point to hoard information, especially those that can increase his control over the outcome. People in modern organizations are not only used to this information hoarding, but have also grown to think that this is the way things should be done. So, even if you are a leader who is willing to share information, your people might not accept it readily. As a leader, you might like your people to get used to it, or to take advantage of it in one go. Unfortunately, it takes longer than that. Truly breaking any glass ceilings should start slowly and proceed slowly, where people feel safe with the information. Where open information is not an uncomfortable aberration to get them, but a good thing to support them, they should feel confident that they will not be harassed because they have accessed some critical information.'

Zaheer Khan, lovingly known as Zach among his colleagues, has been a member of the Indian cricket team since the year 2000. After leading the Indian pace attack for much of the early 2000s, recurring hamstring injuries in 2003 and 2004 forced him out of the team, and after returning for a year, he was dropped again in late 2005. Strong performances on the domestic circuit helped him to be recalled to the team as its leading pace bowler. Zach has now bounced back as one of the top pace bowlers in the world. He says that initially when youngsters including him walked into the team, they had that secret fear of how things would shape up. 'Yes, getting into the team was tough, but after getting in, it was even tougher. When you are playing at the international level, especially immediately after you enter the scene, there is so much pressure, every day, every minute. You do not know whether you would make it or not. At that point of time your greatest need is for information: tips that can help you integrate with the team, tips that can help you take on competition, tips that can help you perform better, tips that can cement your position in the team. Because you will never perform to your fullest, if you do not have the complete idea.

'We were under the impression that seniors would have a lot of airs, especially because overall team positions are limited to eleven, and hence everyone wants to outsmart each other. Why should someone give you tips that could make you more secure in the team and him more insecure? However, that was not the case. Our seniors really went out of their way to make us feel comfortable. In the dressing room and during other functions, they would make an effort to come and talk to us. They would ask about our experience of getting into the Indian side, and how we were progressing. They encouraged us to ask questions, not just relating to matches, but also relating to our insecurities. They were willing to give freely—some of them shared tips on skills that they had acquired through years—knowing pretty well that these could help us improve ourselves drastically and help us score at their expense.'

First step to voice: Giving access to information and making people comfortable with it.

Murli Krishnan suggests that sometimes glass ceilings are automatically created because people perceive a certain distance between themselves and the leader. In the case of Biocon, he says, mitigating this distance was easier when it was smaller. The company initially was focusing on the business-to-business space, where all people were based at a single location. However, this task grew tougher as the company grew larger, with interests in business-to-consumer space, spread out in multiple locations. An employee, unless he was in the top management, would hardly get to meet the leader more than a couple of times a year, that too not individually but in group meetings. This inaccessibility to a leader built the distance. The leader was not a part of them, but someone who was far away from the normal employees—in mindset, in emotions, in perceptions.

The careful use of a leader's space and time can send out important signals about his influence. Hence, in traditional closed organizations, many a time this distance, that separates a leader from his people, is meticulously planned, created and managed. According to Robert Greene, author of *The 48 Laws of Power*, too much circulation makes the value of a leader go down. The more a leader is seen and heard from, the more he appears to be common and less in control. Hence, it becomes important for a traditional closed leader, who relies on power to hold on to his position, to create value through scarcity. The more the hierarchy that separates him from the lowest level, the more powerful he appears to be. The more the physical distance, the more he builds his foundation to be treated as a leader.

'But Kiran,' says Murli, 'is not a typical leader who is trapped in her glasshouse trying to guard her power. She is never in her cabin. She roams around all the time. When she needs something, the easier way for her is to just call the manager in charge and ask him for it, or to just ask her secretary to get her the information. But, she makes sure that she goes directly to the source of the information, rather than relying on middlemen. So, if she needs a detail on production, she would not go to the production manager, but to the technician who actually handles the work.

'Sometimes the physical distance might be just twenty feet between the leader and his people. But the perceived one would be much larger than that. Kiran makes sure that she lessens this by directly going to the source. The advantage is that the person feels immediate proximity to the leader—it is no longer two extremes, it is much closer. He feels connected. More importantly, the person also knows he is responsible and accountable. It is not his manager with whom the ultimate accountability lies, but with him.

'However, Kiran does not stop with this,' continues Murli. 'She employs another method to make people comfortable with the basic philosophy of information sharing to break down glass ceilings. She goes up to people who are handling jobs, and asks them several "why" questions. For example, in the case of a production technician she would ask him things like "Why this target?", "Why is this process followed?" or "Why not something else?" These questions are great conversation creators. It tests the knowledge of the person, it forces him to clarify and more importantly it forces him to ask return questions. And suddenly, it is not just Kiran speaking. It is no longer a one-way conversation, but also a two-way exchange of information. Which is brilliant.'

Vijaya Menon adds in with her bit about Air Deccan. She says Captain Gopinath made an extra effort to remember key details of every part handled by his people, irrespective of management hierarchies. In meetings, most of which were open for anyone to attend, he would randomly pick out a specific point in a project and would drill down. He would encourage, and at times force other members, to ask questions and give feedback in the drill-down process. Or sometimes, when a person was making a power-point presentation, he would ask them to depict the message through another medium—drawing board, flip charts, etc. 'This drill-down and alternative mediums ensure that the information sharing is not just a one-way process, but an interactive and involving exercise. He would ensure that everyone in the conference room was as actively participating as the presenter.'

Arun Chandavarkar tells his side of the story. He says that whenever new employees come into Biocon, he faces reluctance from them in speaking out. First, they are not used to this culture and second they are not aware of the hidden dangers in asking questions. True opinions become elusive in meetings, as most of them are simply keen on agreeing with their seniors. Often, trapped in such a dilemma, Arun resorts to a new trick. In forums of new inductees, Arun reveals information and discusses new ideas freely. However, he takes extra care to make sure that he does not reveal his own position on the subject, or even give the slightest indications about his opinion. He would then ask for their opinions, in a way forcing them to take an independent position. He would also make sure that a person justifies his stand. 'The idea then is not about creating a consensus where everyone agrees with everyone else, but about creating a system where people know that their voicing out does not pose any inherent dangers to their existence in the organization,' says Arun.

Zach completes this note, 'When our seniors came up to us and openly discussed issues, we were encouraged to open a channel of communication with them. We started feeling that seniors were not individuals who were using the system and their experience to their own advantage, but were open people that we can rely on to improve ourselves and improve the team performance.'

> Step two to voice: Force people to talk and to express their opinions by creating channels for two-way communication.

But does this not create insecurity inside the organization because the leader is cutting across the ranks? Murli says it will not, if the organization has nurtured an open environment from the start. He says insecurities will spring up only if one tries to implement this abruptly, especially in places where people are used to a hierarchical environment. 'In most organizations managers play the postman's role, where they waste time acting as a medium of transferring information from one place to another—from the boss to the employees and vice versa. Managers could play much more productive roles, if they are willing to give up their roles as postmen. So, in reality, there is no reason why they should feel insecure. When a leader approaches the source directly, it leaves the manager to focus on bigger responsibilities. Plus, it mitigates a lot of communication gaps and could make the system more efficient.

'But this requires a certain amount of maturity from the part of managers,' continues Murli. 'If the manager is insecure about his position in the company, or if he is using the achievements of his employees just as a means to score brownie points for himself, this will not work. The prerequisite is an environment where everyone feels safe. When Kiran goes directly to my junior to find out some information, say about our bank details, I know perfectly well that she is doing it not because she does not have confidence in me, or to use it against me, but because that makes our teamwork much more productive. I know it is good for me, good for the employee and good for the company. We are all clear on that.'

That in a way sets the platform for a nice two-way communication where employees are not only aware of the minimal distance between them and the leader, but also are aware that all information they require is available—it is just a matter of asking for it.

How Open Source leadership not only gives people their 'voice' but also teaches them to scream

Open Source leadership opens up information preceded by a process that is called capacity building. The underlying assumption is that just allowing people to voice out would not ensure that they would actually voice out. It not only requires a perception change, where people feel safe in voicing out, or access to information, but also an understanding of the information that they are provided with. Voicing can be effective only if people are able to represent their interests adequately through the information that they have access to. However, unfortunately few people, even in established organizations, have these capabilities, since this requires knowledge of rules, resources for defining and articulating positions and experience with negotiation processes, advocacy skills, and specific knowledge of areas like financial documents, accounting and others. In such a scenario, even if a leader decides to share, his people would be in no position to use it because they do not have the know-how. Truly breaking any glass ceiling should start not just with sharing of information, but with helping people learn how to use that information.

The first step towards capacity building is ensuring that people are empowered with more capabilities than just information. For example, at W.L. Gore, they handle this lacuna between information and application through three modes. Firstly by relying on social capital where employees are encouraged to have their old hallway chats and longer water cooler conversations, where they would get opportunities to understand the nuances. Secondly, every employee is associated with a sponsor—a senior in the company who is in no way the boss—who helps out at an informal level. These sponsors act as mentors, giving personal attention, guiding the employees, especially the new ones, in understanding the overall company objectives, team targets and specific expectations from the employee. Armed with a growing understanding of opportunities and team objectives, associates can commit to projects that match their skills. Thirdly, they make sure that they have regular plant communication meetings where leaders share news about company performance with the associates, and walk them through some of the key information areas, especially the tougher ones like financial.

Dawn Anfuso, an award-winning writer and editor, writes about another US company, Springfield Remanufacturing Company, which is into rebuilding engines, generators and other components. Springfield is well known, not only for its openness about information but also for its great capacity building through a highly interesting process. The company runs its day-to-day operations like a game, and even calls it 'The Great Game of Business'.

According to Springfield, they run their business like a game because there are ultimately several similarities between them.

First, the thrill of competition. Businesses like games have competition that they must try to beat with superior market strategies, more talented employees and better products and services. Second, the focus on the scoreboard. As games focus on points or goals, businesses focus on their top line or bottom line. However, similarities end right there. A games captain, aware of the fact that a large part of his success depends on every player, makes efforts in updating everyone about the rules and regulations, not only concerning that person, but also concerning the overall game. Being on the same platform contributes to a team game, and in turn adds to the score. But, in the case of businesses, the enthusiasm for keeping scores is not the same when it comes to understanding of rules are concerned. They need scores, but are not willing to share information.

However, Springfield is different. They strive to make sure that everyone is on the same platform through their rule-sharing sessions. Interestingly, these sessions are not only limited to areas that directly pertain to an employee, but also look into issues that they have no clue about or need not have an interest in. Imagine a technician given access to reams of the overall organizational financial data! In Springfield, rules are always overall rules of the game, and not restricted to specific areas. They understand that, if an individual really needs to play with his full potential, and really needs to get involved in the overall growth of the organization, he should be provided with the big picture, and not partial data.

Springfield teaches players the overall rules of the game, especially an understanding of the financials and of how a business is run. This understanding comes from constant training as well as direct involvement in the concepts. Surprisingly, this education does not wait for a person to settle down and become part of the system or prove his seniority. It begins immediately after the person is hired. During the orientation sessions, each person is given a guidebook that explains every element of business and contains a glossary of terms. Special attention is given to the financial information (a part which most companies hide from everyone else except a closed coterie), because at Springfield they believe that until an employee is able to understand his financial impact on the corporation, he is not really seeing the big picture or really understanding how business works.

Elizabeth Pinchot, co-author of *Intrapreneuring and the End of Bureaucracy and the Rise of the Intelligent Organization*, writes: 'The success of Springfield is based not just on people having a piece of paper that says they are owners, but on the fact that, in addition, people are given tools and the freedom to act like owners. Unless you actually let employee owners in on the decision making and get participative management, worker ownership does not make much difference in the success of the company. At Springfield, ownership means true participation and the tools to intelligently participate.'

Arun Chandavarkar adds on to the Springfield experience as he says that the strangest thing that he noticed whenever he conducted an interview with an outside candidate was the fact the persons were blissfully unaware of what was going on in the organization even a level above or below them. This is rather peculiar for Arun, because he comes from an environment where nothing is hidden from the eyes of an employee—even finances that pertain to their departments. From the time an employee walks in, he is given access to confidential secrets. No information, no topic is a taboo. People know how much it costs them to make a product and what contribution an individual brings to the table—be it in R&D department or in sales. Everything is put into an overall perspective. People, at whatever level they are, are empowered completely with all the information and tools they need, so that they feel part of the decision-making process.

Step one to scream: Undertake capacity building, where people can appreciate overall business, and not just their restricted fields.

However, shattering of glass ceilings does not stop at capacity building—where people are given access to information and are guided to decipher the complexities inherent in them. It has to go on to truly enable people—to really help them use information and capacities for productive results. Most Open Source leadership organizations follow a three-step process towards this: expecting people to be both responsible and accountable with the information given, giving them space to operate without too many interferences, and giving them the credit for what is done.

'It is not that we were given tips on how to perform and were left in the open. Sourav made it a point to clearly define what was expected of us so that each one of us could contribute to the victory,' says Bhajji. 'He made it a point to reiterate what was expected out of each player as a batsman, as a bowler and as a fielder. There was no ambiguity in his expectations. For example, he used to tell me that I would be stepping in during these overs, when the scenario might be this and hence these would be the expectations. If the actual scenario turned out to be different from what was expected, we would rework, even if that meant on the go. But overall, I knew where my standing in the team was, what to expect and where the team was headed.

'At the same time what really worked out was the fact that he kept things simple. Once the overall team goals and individual roles were agreed upon, it was a given that people would own up their responsibilities. The captain need not be behind them; they would work towards fulfilling them. When you are playing international cricket that is the minimum that is expected out of you—that you are mature enough to know what you are supposed to do. You might be as young as eighteen years old, but you are expected to be responsible.'

Ramesh Rao, the camp coordinator at Bangalore agrees with Bhajji on this point. He says that Ganguly understood the fact that team performance was important but at the same time also understood that coordinated individual performance was actually what a team performance was all about. And hence, defining a role for each player and conveying it were of utmost importance, as much as defining overall team targets. He says, in the team meetings, whether these were before the match or after the first session, Ganguly would be vocal of what was expected out of each player.

Having seen Ganguly operate during several matches, Rao thinks there are two merits in conveying individual expectations out in the open rather than in private. Firstly, it would help the player clearly understand his place in the team. Each person gets the message that his individual performance matters as much, and hence there is no way he could hide himself behind team performances. Secondly, it helps others to frame their own strategies and to coordinate their performances to their fellow players, since now every role is defined. And thirdly, it helps give credit where it is due. People who have lived up to expectations stand out, irrespective of a win or a loss.

> Step two to scream: Convey expectations from each individual clearly—in private as well as in public.

'But then someone holding you responsible is very different from feeling responsible yourself. Real results will start coming out when roles are clarified and space is given to you to fulfil those roles. There is no point in defining roles, but not giving space to accomplish. Don't you think that again is a kind of glass ceiling?' questions Vijaya Menon from Air Deccan.

N. Vaghul, the former chairman of ICICI Bank says that though they managed to induct people based on their merit, sans any other bias including gender, they soon came face to face with another hurdle—the traditional work environment—filled with gender biases to the brim. It was designed to meet the needs of men and completely ignored the special requirements of women.

ICICI Bank decided to walk the full length by redesigning the workplace. That did not mean taking away anything from the current environment, but adding additional features to suit the new members. Women have child-bearing responsibilities, so they decided to be liberal and give them more than the mandatory three months' maternity leave. Women also have additional responsibilities of nurturing children. If someone wanted eight to ten months off, it was sanctioned. They created a working environment that was also women-friendly. The results were soon to come by, as women became more loyal towards the organization, helping the bank's growth during a crucial period—the early days of the Indian economic reform process—even as other banks struggled with high employee turnover.

Vijaya Menon comments that Air Deccan was devoid of any glass ceilings because Captain Gopi not only expected his people to perform, but also facilitated the performance by not standing in the way of their freedom. She says he not only never interfered, but also did not let others interfere. 'Gopi lets people take their own decisions. However, do not let that fool you because you can never get cosy or comfortable when you are responsible for your own decisions. Responsibility also means accountability. You are committed to it. You are hyperactive all the time, because you are thinking about ways in which you could reach your goal. In Air Deccan most of the innovations came about because we were all responsible for solving our problems. We were responsible for our actions.'

Sandeep Bhargava of Studio18 narrates an incident from his previous professional life to drive home this point. While he was at Mudra Communications, a large advertising firm in India, his boss resigned. Sandeep felt that he was the best candidate, even as the firm scouted around for a replacement. Of course, his experience was much less than what was required, nevertheless Sandeep believed that he would be able to do more justice to the position than any outsider. As he went ahead and put forward his proposal to the branch head, he was given a simple proposition: 'During the next thirty days prove to me that you are capable of meeting all the requirements of your clients. Make sure that you take care of them in such a way that none of them feel the need to contact me.' Sandeep managed to prove his point in twenty-one days flat and his branch head, as promised, handed over to him senior responsibilities. In those twenty-one days, Sandeep tells us that his branch head never interfered on how he was going about it. He was supported, and at the same time he was given a free rein on how he would like to approach the challenge. 'That did the trick,' comments Sandeep.

'If my branch manager did not give me that chance, he would have ended up hiring a manager above me, who would do nothing more than managing me. That would have demotivated me thoroughly. At the same time, if my manager kept on interfering in all my decisions, after challenging me, that again would have defeated the purpose because I would be able to take up true responsibility only if he took his hands off. I learnt much from that incident. Especially about giving people a free hand. I am now a fairly hands-off leader, where I really keep myself off consciously from day-to-day operations. I make sure that once goals are agreed upon, I stay far away from the modus operandi of the person. They might end up doing things in a completely different way, probably even not to my liking. But so what? I have learnt from my experience that the only way to put pressure on a person and to make him accountable is to give him all the freedom to achieve his goals.'

During those twenty-one days, Sandeep handled the biggest clients of Mudra—Reliance Industries and Vimal Suitings—all by himself. He was a junior, yet the trust was intact that he could handle it as good as any other senior. At the same time, freedom also meant freedom to do things his way, even if that meant learning from his mistakes.

Senthil Chengalvarayan, whose full name is Nammudi Vellasithan Sinnaiah Senthil Chengalvarayan, probably one of the longest names in the history of the world media, is currently president and editorial director of TV18, a part of Network18. He narrates an incident from his early days with the company, the initial stages of TV18, when the office had nothing more than a bunch of youngsters, fresh out of college. There were twenty-six of them, all working on various small and insignificant assignments. Then, TV18 happened to win an assignment with the BBC—the India Business Report. The assignment was not only critical but also strategic. Critical because they had by then lost a contract with Doordarshan, the state-owned television operator, their bread and butter. Strategic because Raghav knew well that this show would be their ticket to high places when the Indian television industry opened up. Yet, Raghav decided it would be these youngsters who would again be involved in the new programme. Some senior would not be brought in to take their place just because the assignment was bigger. Raghav gave them opportunities and support—as far as they could go. And that drove home the point, so much so that the young chaps got to work right away. Never before had they worked harder, because they realized that they carried a huge responsibility on their shoulders. They would shoot for almost ten hours, and would edit another five hours—all for a mere five-minute capsule. The result was a brilliant show, almost the finest to be produced—making that programme a case study of sorts, to the point that it became the longest-running privately produced programme for the BBC.

A decisive factor that contributed to the excellence in the programming was the freedom and support which Raghav gave these youngsters, even when the future of his company was at stake. To demonstrate the point further, Senthil narrates another incident, this time with Doordarshan, for whom TV18 produced a business show. During those times, live shows were just a distant dream. Hence, business shows were recorded on cassettes and sent to the television channel office, a few hours before the airing time, for the officials to review.

Once a young journalist from TV18, who went to deliver the cassette, got into an argument with an official over some content which he took an objection to. The journalist thought that the official's objections were unfounded. Raghav was asked to intervene. The easiest thing for Raghav to do, considering the fact that the show was important, was to support the official, to apologize and to move forward. However, Raghav chose to stand by his person. The incident ended up costing him the contract. The message was loud and clear—at TV18, people would not only have their set of responsibilities but also would have their own secure space to play.

The true breaking of glass ceilings is not just about delegating responsibilities, but also about giving them space to work and supporting them truly in whatever they choose to do. Because not supporting your people after giving them freedom is again a sort of glass ceiling, wherein you are sending a subtle message—that you expect things to be done your way, for your purpose.

'We promote TV18 in such a way that there are no glass ceilings. Only talent should matter here, not age, not experience, not anything else,' says Senthil. To demonstrate his point better, he points out to a young chap who sits right next to his workstation. 'He has just about four to five years' experience but occupies a position that would take any traditional journalist about fifteen years. Why? Because he is sharp and is able to thrive in a non-political environment devoid of glass ceilings. We do not hold him by the hand anymore, because we know that he is able to operate on his own. Yes, mistakes do happen, because he is trying out new ideas. But these mistakes never get repeated, because people are given a responsible and accountable environment.'

Step three to scream: Give people their space to operate without too many interferences.

However, the challenge does not end there. Many organizations claim that there is unlimited growth. However, the writing on the wall is clear: a subordinate is not supposed to be better than the superior. If he is, let him better use his talents to contribute to the growth of the superior. Which means you might be given the freedom to explore, but if you come up with something good, someone senior shall take the credit. Voice, accountability and freedom take care of a large part—making sure that credit goes where it is really due. At the same time, Open Source leadership also makes sure that there is a proper process in place, which can assert the importance of credits.

At Springfield they focus on their top line and bottom line as if they are scores on a game. However, what keeps it exciting is also the fact that it is not only the results that people are striving to achieve, but also the individual rewards that are attached to them. The scoring is not in vain but has dollars linked to it. The most tangible of these is the company's bonus programme, appropriately called 'Skip the Praise, Give Us the Raise', where people are assessed against their performances not yearly but almost every week. In fact, at Springfield, the primary purpose of capacity building is to make sure that their people clearly know how to define their priorities. Hence, the last stage of capacity building is what they call a 'Huddle', normally on a Tuesday afternoon or a Wednesday morning. Here people share how they have performed over the last week. This performance is then directly compared against a scorecard that is maintained by a manager. However, managers do not drive the meeting, they merely validate the performances to ensure minimum amount of subjectivity. The process makes sure that there is maximum transparency, not only regarding the results but also in the credits. Moreover, defining the frequency for these meetings as weekly ensures that any subjectivity that can creep in with delayed evaluation is taken off. At Springfield, it does not matter who you are or whom you work for. If you have done work on a project, you would get the credit—for sure.

At W.L. Gore, the rules for rewards try to smash any remaining glass ceilings. It does not matter to which group a person belongs, because you are always allowed and expected to cut across and go to whomever to get things done. In fact, at times it so happens that star sales people are often requested to help out in territories that are doing not so well. Yes, it would damage these stars' own bottom line, because they are now investing their efforts on other territories. However, they do not mind doing this, because the organizational system is equipped to capture contributions in the truest sense. People need not be afraid to take risks, because rewards are related not only to their direct contributions, but also to their indirect contributions to the overall long-term success of the company.

Anindya Banerjee comments that a good process becomes all the more critical as organizations grow. He says, back in 1996, ICICI Bank had just about one thousand employees, and hence it was easy to make sure that every person got his due, even without a greatly structured process. But now with tens of thousands of employees, it is a much more difficult process to keep control over, and almost impossible if they did not have a thorough and evolved process in place. So, ICICI Bank has evolved a 360-degree evaluation process to ensure that there are minimal glass ceilings as far as rewards are concerned. Every employee goes through this process, where he gets to talk about not only his achievements but also his entire professional sphere—including his boss, his peers and his goals. A structured questionnaire makes sure that every nuance is captured in the most objective manner, and qualitative input ensures that personal details are not missed out. This is complemented with another two-tier programme—a leadership assessment programme, where potential leaders are picked out by peers and a talent assessment programme, where managers pick out subordinates who show superior talent. There are also several panels that act complementary, where people spend several hours together discussing, evaluating and appraising their superiors, peers and subordinates.

Anindya believes that this is an effective way to evaluate and reward, simply because of the fact that it is multidimensional—in terms of the tools and the people that would assess a person. Hence, subjectivity, even if it creeps in at one stage, could be eliminated in the next. The person would get a fair assessment of the things that he has done, that the credits are given to where it is really due.

Step four to scream: Ensure credit to where it is really due.

Corporate cultures based on Open Source leadership have realized that walking the talk of creating a workplace free of any inherent glass ceilings can truly transform their organizations. They realize that most people would go any length to earn the trust that is given to them. And by showing unconditional trust instead of barriers, people will not only take ownership and accountability, but would also dig deeper into themselves to reveal their full potential. Of course, there could be a few bad apples. However, penalizing everyone else for the failures of a few should not be made the rule. Open Source leadership believes that everyone wants to be great, they trust them to do great things and create an environment that could enable them to do those.

Randy Spitzer, co-author of the book *Accountability: Freedom and Responsibility without Control* suggests some quick rules to live by:

1. Become a values-driven organization: Make it safe for everyone in the organization to strive to their fullest potential than just playing to the whims and fancies of their bosses. Insist that everyone in the organization be bias-free. Always create an environment where access to opportunities are equal, purely based on talent, regardless of positions.

2. Create a safe environment: Create an environment where sharing ideas that may be politically unpopular can be expressed freely and appropriately, where everyone can be honest about what they think and how they feel. Celebrate new ideas, even if they seem to go against the grain, in the name of experimentation and innovation. Make it safe to ask for help or mentoring whenever needed, regardless of rank or role in the organization.

3. Expect people to be both responsible and accountable: Expect everyone in the organization to be fully responsible and accountable for doing their jobs without the need for supervision and show appreciation for what each individual contributes.

4. Encourage everyone to do their best: Expect people on the front lines to design, monitor and measure the processes and systems within which they work, encourage continuous improvement through constant experimentation.

5

Unleashing a Horse with No Blinders
Open Source Leadership Opens up the Organizational Vision to Everyone

In this section:
- How the Brazilian city of Porto Alegre opened its treasuries to the public
- How people on the shop floor, sales and customer service can move from cogs in the wheel to drivers of the giant wheel
- Why Open Source leadership visions tend to be fuzzier and vague in a world where we are fighting for clarity
- How open leaders instigate average people to come up with extraordinary visions

How the Brazilian city of Porto Alegre opened its treasuries to the public

Brazil, just a few decades back, was the seat of authoritarian politics, where an oligarchic, patrimonial state led by a few individuals, shadowed over its people, stifling their rights and participation. 'But the scene changed,' writes Boaventura de Sousa Santos, a professor of sociology at the School of Economics, University of Coimbra (Portugal), 'as one of the political parties—The Workers Party—founded in the early eighties out of the labour movement, started gaining strength.' After winning local elections in several cities in Brazil, important among them being Porto Alegre, they started a wave of open and democratic innovations—enabling common citizens to share and participate in larger goals that concerned them—starting from defining goals to its implementation.

103

One of these was 'participatory budgeting', aimed at guaranteeing popular participation in the definition as well as preparation of the municipal budget (thought of to be a complex area to be handled only by a select set of individuals possessing specialized skills), and hence in the distribution of resources and investment priorities.

However, this was not an easy process, considering the fact that most people were marginalized from high-profile decisions until then. Broad rules were framed, preparatory meetings were held, and municipal authorities communicated all the technical recommendations in words that would be easily understood by the people. Citizens, in turn, set goals for their communities, and assigned priorities for developmental work in their region.

Participatory budgeting broke the till then entrenched thinking that ordinary citizens could not effectively participate and do justice to exercises that involved big-picture thinking. It ensured that people at all levels could not only buy into a larger vision, but could also effectively participate in the making of it. The process did wonders to the way communities were subsequently managed in Brazil—middle-class participation increased, and the city was virtually free of corruption, improving the general services particularly cherished by the middle classes such as garbage collection, public spaces, gardens and parks, and cultural activities. Not only this, the whole mobilization and public discourse around urban issues even enhanced the self-esteem and morale of the city as a whole, an elusive but nonetheless crucial symbolic urban value.

How people on the shop floor, sales and customer service can move from cogs in the wheel to drivers of the giant wheel

Traditional leadership thrived on the old Brazil philosophy—Brazil before the Porto Alegre experiment—where there was a person who would lead the overall vision, and a majority who would blindly work on an opaque block of bits to convert that vision into reality. Those who worked on these small portions, almost certainly, were never exposed to the vision in its entirety. People on the shop floor, sales, customer service—all became cogs in the giant wheel, where they never got a view of the whole wheel as such. However, Open Source leadership reflected the participative budgeting exercise in many ways. Here, every team member was as much part of a shared goal as they were of its implementation. Nobody was working blindly on a small task, without perspective, but everyone knew how they fitted in and where they fitted in.

As a young PhD student, Arun Chandavarkar was in India to learn more about the opportunities in the biotechnology sector. Kiran Mazumdar Shaw, more than anyone else in the industry, took extra efforts to sketch for him what Biocon stood for and what it was striving to do—why they were in the area of enzymes, how they would set up world-class innovation centres, and how they would grow by focusing on India. For Arun, this immediately brought in a connect between what the company was doing and wanted to do and what he wanted to achieve in life—he shared the goal and wholeheartedly believed in it. This eased out his decision-making process, especially since it was a tough one between a systematic US and chaotic India, and between the large R&D facilities of Unilever and the small start-up Biocon.

Helping people share a larger goal and taking pains in ensuring that they buy into it are an integral part of the Open Source leadership model. There are two advantages in this. First, it helps people align their interests to the larger interests of the organization. Hence, they would be in a position to take more informed decisions than the ones where they are given less information, like in the case of Arun who decided to join Biocon, in spite of the bigger offers he received. At the same time, adherence to a larger goal also helps people to justify and offer sacrifices when required, even at the cost of personal gains. For example, in W.L. Gore people jointly decide many a time not to hire additional help, even if that means each one of them has to sacrifice more of his or her personal time. Because they adhere to a larger vision, they are willing to volunteer help to even other departments or colleagues.

John Shaw is Scottish by birth. He was the chairman of Madura Coats when he met Kiran for the first time in Bangalore. Those were busy days for both of them—John was busy managing his company, while Kiran was busy setting up her biotechnology initiative. Though initially John paid little attention, he was eventually attracted by Kiran's passion and enthusiasm towards her venture. He was impressed by the clarity of her vision and the future she was building.

He not only appreciated Kiran's passion, he decided to share it too. He invested in the vision that he believed in by buying shares in her company. However, it was soon time for John to return to Europe. Meanwhile, Kiran was suddenly in a dilemma. Unilever, which was one of the promoters in her company, decided to sell their stake. Kiran either had to raise enough funds to buy back Unilever's share, or give up on her dreams. John could help, but that called for a sacrifice—either follow his original plan of going back to Europe or decide to go with Kiran's vision. John went back to Europe—however, not to settle down in his comfort zone, but to sell his house and other valuables in order to fund Kiran on her journey. 'It was not a favour. I believed that the vision belonged to me as much as it did for Kiran,' says John proudly.

Vasudhi had done her MBA in marketing and was working with Sify, an Internet company, when she happened to spend some time at the Art of Living campus. She immediately noticed several differences between the professional atmosphere, one that she was used to, and the ashram. In a multinational environment, she says, everything is a given. You have access to required resources and are surrounded by competent colleagues. She was surprised seeing a laid-back ashram, where nothing could be taken for granted. Everything depended on your relationship with the other person than on sheer professionalism. She could not grasp how a system could function like this, as she observed it through her conventional wisdom.

As Vasudhi met up with Sri Sri Ravi Shankar, the founder, she got a ringside view of what they have been trying to achieve. She could then easily put things into perspective. It lacked the comforts that she was used to, but she could relate to these ideals nevertheless. Once she bought in to these, it was easier for her to decide where she actually belonged. Vasudhi quit her job, her plum salary and her obsession with a multinational career. Currently, she is a volunteer in the ashram, a state teacher-coordinator, travelling around to the deepest and most interior villages in Karnataka, often in the most challenging situations, dealing with people who have never ever been close to a professional atmosphere.

Through her story, Vasudhi has brought out an important point of discussion: On why sharing and common ownership of vision is not just desirable but a necessity for Open Source leadership organizations. It assumes importance from two angles. First, from a resource perspective, Open Source leadership organizations often start from a position of weakness. An organization like Biocon, in its start-up phase, or a charitable institution like Art of Living, have little access to valuable resources compared to an established competitor. Being small and ridden with weaknesses as a physical entity, they could easily lose out, unless they were willing to change the game itself. If it happens to be one where people can own it and play a larger-than-life role, it becomes easier to get attention. And it becomes easier to attract resources. Second, from a culture fit perspective, for Open Source leadership organizations, challenge does not stop with attracting resources—they have to attract the right resources. Wrong resources could have long-term implications—misuse of common systems, abuse of freedom and sometimes even complete neglect of the open culture. Sharing of vision and spending enough time to let people buy in play a large part in ensuring that the right people are coming in and blending in.

Step one towards enabling people to be drivers of a giant wheel: Share your vision. Spend enough personal time to make people buy in.

Although many organizations start their journey like this, they soon lose their way. Because it is easier to spend personal time and ensure people buy in to a vision while you are a small organization, but extremely difficult as you grow large. However, holding on to this shared vision concept is the key to Open Source leadership. And organizations like ICICI and Art of Living have proved that they can get every one of their people to buy in—even as they have grown in size to tens of thousands of employees/members. How do they do this?

Chanda Kochhar says that at ICICI Bank, the culture was set in place right from the initial days—where leaders spend adequate time with each one of their people to ensure buy-in. At the same time, vision sharing was also not a task restricted to the leadership level. It was shared across levels through many ways—formal and conscious sharing through platforms like organizational meetings, conferences etc. and through informal subconscious mechanisms like unofficial chit-chats. Since the organization was closely knit during the initial days, every conversation, every task was translated automatically into a vision-sharing session. 'But, as we grew larger, we faced the same dilemma as most other organizations: many levels, many hierarchies, many roles.'

A large organization is filled with hierarchies. In traditional closed organizations, apart from the management control function, hierarchies also perform an information-sieving function—sieving that happens in two ways. In the upward sieving, the top level makes sure that the lower levels are reaching out to them only with critical information and not flooding them with everything that is happening on the ground. In the downward sieving, the management makes sure that they are passing on only the really required information for the lower levels to perform their tasks. All strategic information is sieved out.

However, in Open Source leadership, this sieving defeats the purpose. It leads to loss of information, much valued in these organizations. Every level conveys to the other level information after lots of sieving, coloured by its own subjectivity. Ultimately, what reaches out to the last link would be far removed from the real vision itself. That defeats the purpose.

'In a large organization like ICICI Bank, where we have close to 2,000 branches and more than 50,000 employees we can never assume that people would pick up the vision automatically. Sharing the big picture cannot be done merely through some memos or occasional meetings. It has to be done on a continuous basis. A leader along with his senior team has to get out there, and spend a lot of time sharing the detailed vision with every cross section of employees. They have to focus not only on the numbers that the company is planning to achieve, but also on details like where they want to be, why they are striving to be in this place and what is the role of each person in creating such a future.

'Easier said than done. But how would you do this?' Chanda continues, 'It is easy to talk about vision sharing, sitting inside the corner office. And share bits and pieces whenever your people pass by your office. But if you are really serious about it, you have to invert this pyramid. A leader has to go to the places where his smallest employee is based. A leader has to go to him, rather than expecting him to come to the leader.'

Chanda connects it to her personal experience. 'I used to travel to branch offices across the country almost twice a week. I would cover four to five branches in a day. In each of these branches, I would do three things to reiterate our vision. First, I would tell them the vision as it is—this is where your bank is going, this is the kind of progress that we have achieved in the last few years. I would also sketch before them the actual contribution that their branch has made to this overall vision. This puts things in perspective—that you are not just a person who is working in a remote branch thousands of miles away from the headquarters, but actually contributing substantially and positively. But, this telling of the vision is just half the job done. Because how much ever effective this telling is, there still is a certain amount of subjectivity attached, depending upon the person. Especially in a business such as ours where a lot of big picture perception is dependent on one small picture—customer service. I could go on and on about this to the employee, but he would never understand the gravity completely until I demonstrated to him what this meant to the company. An irate customer might look like a trivial aspect from the perspective of a big company for an employee. He could easily assume that he could afford to lose him with no real loss to the company. It is not so.

'Hence, I resort to the actual demonstration of where we want to be—through video clippings of real-life incidents. So there is this employee who has been listening to me till now on the ten steps to a better customer experience, but the minute he sees a video of a real incident in a branch similar to his, about one of the hundreds of customers that he meets in a day, the reality sinks in. He takes away a real learning that contributes to the real organizational vision.

'My vision-sharing session does not stop there. People still have some gaps in their understanding and perception, and I need to close that loop. So, I resort to a third step, which is reiteration of the vision. Here the employees narrate their version of the vision back to me: what does it mean for them, what are the challenges, what are the other opportunities. That really hardens the foundation of the shared vision.

'There is another beautiful aspect to this third step. That it reiterates the vision not only for your people, but for the leader too. A leader can construct his vision in the glasshouse, but he does not understand how it all fits in on a ground scenario, until he gets into the shoes of his junior-level people. It is easy for a leader to believe the data and the numbers that are coming in, but once he is exposed to the ground realities, the experience is never the same. At the same time, from an employee's perspective, listening to his version of the vision and making an effort to be in his shoes means a lot to him. That the leader is not the sole monopoly over the organizational vision, but it belongs to them also. That the leader is not pushing a fully developed vision down their throat, but is actually involved in a process of constructing a vision alongside every other employee.

'Hence, vision sharing becomes a different exercise altogether. It is no longer a one-way but a two-way street, where it is constructed together, brick by brick, taking into consideration the realities and opinions of every person involved. And only then is the ownership of the vision truly complete.'

> Step two towards enabling people to be drivers of a giant wheel: Vision is not a concept that has one version. Everyone has a version. So, make vision sharing a two-way process. Get into their shoes. Understand their version of the vision.

Why Open Source leadership visions tend to be fuzzier and vague in a world where we are fighting for clarity

In a world where we are used to traditional closed leadership, vision that emerges from all across an organization is almost unthinkable. Would it not result in mayhem if people came from everywhere and started chipping in with their two cents of wisdom?

Interestingly, in Open Source leadership, vision defining does not work the usual way. 'What is the final goal of a corporation?' Prof. Balram, director of IISc asks. 'It is to maximize the profit for investors. It tends to be very refined and clear. There are defined boundaries for such goals. For example, Infosys will not diversify into pharmaceuticals tomorrow. Because their goal is different and is defined within a territory.'

Open Source leadership organizations are different. While typical corporate goals are more purposeful, Open Source leadership goals are much fuzzier and broader. Quite often, there are no real well-defined boundaries as such. A good example is a research institution like IISc. Here the real goal or even the vision is to be able to claim the individual success of its people in the spheres that they have chosen to succeed in—to be recognized for the work of your faculty, the work of your students.

In Open Source leadership, every individual person is on a mission—to explore and find his own goal. This is different from one single collective goal as defined by a corporate. Often, in Open Source leadership, the institution as such does not restrict individual goals within a boundary, quite unlike a corporation that defines your area of operation—as a marketing person or as a sales person. Prof. Balram suggests that this process is very much similar to a sports person who chooses his event based on his own evaluation of strengths and weaknesses. There is no external compulsion for the person to choose an event. It is an individual choice.

'In the same manner, you could choose your research area in IISc—electrical engineering, organic chemistry, sustainable development or anything else. But once you choose, it is your personal responsibility to keep going and to excel. As an institution, I cannot push you directly to excel because there are several organizational limitations. The only thing we could probably do is to create an environment where you yourself would want to excel, like great research facilities, great peer support or mentorship. At the same time, if you do not define your goals, or you do not reach the goals that you have set for yourself, the institution cannot do much about it. It cannot explicitly penalize you, other than the guilt that you would carry around. It is an open system in every way. Even goals tend to be open for you to define,' says Prof. Balram.

Boston Consulting Group or BCG, as it is popularly known, is as much a blue-blooded management consultancy as it can get. Among the myriad of consultancies, BCG stands apart on a number of dimensions. It has an unparalleled record of innovation, examples of which include portfolio analysis, experience curves, segmentation, time-based competition, and deconstruction—models familiar to every management graduate.

BCG in its daily operations tries to combine an entrepreneurial spirit with individual talent—each project offering new opportunities to create entirely new ways of thinking—one of the reasons why they believe several of their alumni are successful in their own spheres. Dr Janmejaya Sinha, who holds a master's degree in economics from Cambridge, UK, and a PhD from Princeton University's Woodrow Wilson School, USA, is the chairman of the Asia region.

Dr Sinha compares the goal-creation process in an Open Source leadership organization to a journey vis-à-vis a destination in conventional ones. Whereas a destination can be defined clearly and could be a certainty, a journey is less so. For a destination, only one definition is possible. You know it when you reach it. However, a journey is more flexible and open. It can accommodate different perspectives and can even continue forever, as long as people who are travelling are willing.

Step three towards enabling people to be drivers of a giant wheel: Focus on a journey that can accommodate individual perspectives rather than a destination that is rigid and predefined.

Dr Sinha looks at the specific case of BCG, where people join a journey rather than a set of predefined corporate objectives. Here, individual aspirations take precedence. More than what they want to do for BCG, it looks at how personal aspirations can be accommodated. BCG as an organization knows that as long as people exhibit a few traits like passion, curiosity and an ambition to change the world, they would fit in and can join the journey. However, he also cautions that such an organization can fall apart if it does not offer 'enough space' to accommodate all individual aspirations.

'When I say "enough space" to accommodate all, I really mean a large space in every manner,' says Dr Sinha. 'For example, specific positions tend to be limited in supply in conventional organizations. This limited supply means people have to compete to get to these, which in a way imposes restrictions upon them. However, unlike in normal organizations, positions and designations are not in limited supply here. In a normal organization, there cannot be more than one operations director, while in BCG there are no limits to the numbers who could be partners. There is no one CEO spot. Everyone can be a partner. Everyone's ambitions could be accommodated.

'This large space to play around is not developed by random chance, but by a clear choice, considering the challenges in the industry that we operate in. Consulting tends to be a supply-driven business and not a demand-driven one. If you are good, there is infinite demand for you, but if you are bad there is zero demand for you. So a sure-fire way by which you can be good is by attracting good people and by keeping them with you. Good people tend to be ambitious and cannot be restricted. If you put a large number of ambitious people together, without offering them enough opportunities and space to play, the whole premise would crumble down. Individual egos could start trampling upon each other, or people could get exasperated out of the chasm between talk and practice. Hence, it is important to have a larger space.

'At the same time,' he continues, 'ambitious people are like a herd of cats. You cannot dictate your point of view, quite unlike in a conventional organization, where you could have one goal driven directly by a CEO. In an open environment, all you can do is to just show them a perspective and be persuasive enough to allow them to engage with your perspective—not necessarily agree with you, but engage with you. Your only chance of influence is to align with them on an agreed path.'

Step four towards enabling people to be drivers of a giant wheel: Offer a large enough playing space to accommodate all individual aspirations. Engage and align together in this space.

How open leaders instigate average people to come up with extraordinary visions

Not all Open Source leadership organizations are like the IISc or BCG, where only the most brilliant and ambitious get through. Ambitious individuals are mature and focused enough to develop individual goals of their own and pursue them, which could ultimately add value to the whole system as such. However, organizations like Art of Living or Air Deccan are completely different. In Art of Living, for example, the organization has no control over the kind of people who come in—some might be brilliant among them, but most are just average. While in the case of Air Deccan, the very principle of low cost itself restricted them from having access to the best paid in the industry.

This lands some of the Open Source leadership organizations in a dilemma. Because most of these average joes who come in are neither ambitious nor brilliant, they have no idea, even about their aspirations, or on how to control their destiny. Most of them are more comfortable serving in troops, being one of the faces in a crowd, than taking on any larger role as such. Some of them might not even be interested in the creation of a shared vision or its implementation.

'This is exactly where the role of a leader comes in,' says Vikram Hazra. 'The leader has to be sensitive enough in understanding his people, and knowing what could incentivize them to follow a personal goal. In Art of Living, guruji does not accept anything blindly, just because you are volunteering. If someone comes up and wants to be a teacher, he questions him on why he wants to do that. It is not a passing or a casual question. He expects them to actively search for an answer and get back to him in probably ten days or so. In these ten days, you are walking around with that question plugged in your mind, meditating over it and talking to others about it. By the end of it all, you have better clarity—you know for sure whether this is what you want or something else.'

Step one towards instigating people towards extraordinary visions: Be sensitive enough to understand your people, and at the same time question intentions.

Vikram Hazra continues to delve even more deeply into the issue by bringing in specific examples.

'People think that they can give up on all personal ambitions just because it is an ashram. Not so. Here in fact the search gets more intensified. A good story is that of Naveena, who was an intern helping guruji with some of our Ayurveda projects. But guruji did not want her to stop at researching with purely academic goals. He encouraged her to think about the next level, to explore opportunities with the research she was doing. She came back with some Ayurvedic product samples, which ended up getting some excellent appreciation. Now we have a complete manufacturing set-up. Naveena discovered her inner passion and this added to the overall vision of the ashram. Now, it is not just a place where spiritual knowledge is imparted. We also cater to the medical and cosmetic needs of our people, rooted in the same values that we are trying to propagate.

'Harish has done his BTech from IIT Mumbai and was very comfortable in his teacher's role at Art of Living. But again, guruji would not accept that. He would instigate him, "Your parents have invested so much in your education but you are content with your routine tasks. Our country, your parents, and this ashram cannot afford to waste an IIT seat. So, you have to think beyond." That forced Harish out of his comfort zone to search for something that could put his learning to good use. He came up with this idea of information security. Today Sumeru Technology, which is part of the ashram, is one of the few organizations that do security verification for Microsoft products. It is Harish's personal goal, yet it adds immensely to the vision of the ashram—it makes us self-sustainable, it attracts more educated people and it supports the development of the system as a whole.

'But sometimes it is not as simple as this. In the case of Naveena and Harish it worked because they already had defined a broad sphere for themselves to play in. In the majority of cases, they do not even know where they fit in. They come to the ashram and expect the leader to command them into a role.

'Interestingly, guruji plays the role of an awakener here. He opens up our mind by helping to simplify complexities, opening our eyes to the imperceptible and by providing perspectives. For example, every time we drive from one village to another, he makes sure that he points out to us all those subtle changes that have happened from our last visit and relates it to a larger picture—say, "Look at that new building and the new shops that have come up." That means there is something positive happening about the economy of this place. Is it good or bad, or is it something that we should take care of? He asks us to be open and vigilant, even about smaller things that can open our eyes to our real potential. So when a volunteer is sent to a village to serve as the Art of Living teacher, what is really expected out of him is a larger role—in the development of that village itself.'

Vijaya Menon agrees with this. 'Captain Gopi plays a similar role in making sure that every one of us, irrespective of our potential, is up to speed. He simplifies complexities as much as possible, so that we can absorb not just the details that are required for our roles, but how each one of us can actively contribute towards the goal.

'I personally find two things that he does extremely interesting. He always makes sure to capture things in a visual diagram, trying to give us complex details in the simplest manner, so that even someone in the lowest rung can understand easily. Another thing is that he always makes it a point to start every conversation right from the beginning, so that everyone knows what is going on—in its entirety. For example, if we are discussing a new service in the airline, he does not talk just about the service alone, but how the idea evolved. He makes sure that you understand the entire context, not just what you are supposed to do. That ensures that people are in charge. You are not only responsible for your part of the work, but for the success of the whole thing. He aligns you to the overall vision and then asks you to add your part to it.'

Chanda Kochhar has another interesting perspective on how ICICI Bank prepares their youngsters in the art of visualizing. She says that the leadership at the bank always encouraged its people to see the unseen, to anticipate what is going to happen, rather than just being reactive to events. She gives the example of the sprawling retail business of ICICI Bank, which less than a couple of decades ago was almost unthinkable in India. Retail lending as an industry was non-existent since Indians were not used to a borrowing culture, and the per capita income was stuck at a low US$500. But ICICI Bank would not mistake the present for the future. People were asked to look at other country case studies, analyse trends and construct scenarios on how consumer behaviour would change, as the country progressed. As people went into these data points, suddenly they could see the future. They could see what they should be doing. The vision was right in front of the eyes of those who thought they would remain cogs in the wheel.

At the same time they had a choice either to just remain mentally ready for the future they predicted, or to go ahead and physically create that market and need. ICICI Bank prepared their people to embrace the second step. The bank's leadership supported its people as they engaged in changing the financial landscape of the nation. Some of these even carried big risks—like the roll-out of ATMs. At that point of time, the whole nation had just around 300 ATMs, built through several decades. However, ICICI Bank decided that they would go ahead and set up another

2,000 ATMs across the nation during the next eighteen months, to prepare for the consumerist wave, or rather to welcome it. Therefore, the vision that the people generated did not remain just on paper—the bank had the conviction to go ahead and convert that into reality.

> Step two towards instigating people towards extraordinary visions: Simplify a world of complexities for your people. Open their eyes to see the unseen.

'At the same time, guruji does not leave his people alone once he has simplified complexities and provided perspectives. Because he understands that a person could still be stranded. So, he also goes ahead and plays the role of a facilitator. He makes sure that people are connected to the right opportunities and resources so that they can take their expanded thinking to the next level,' suggests Vikram.

'When people go to him with their ideas, he connects them to people who could help them. Like this young chap Karan, who was working in the human resources department in a company before coming to the Art of Living. He had identified that there was an opportunity in giving mentoring support to youngsters who were preparing for their job interviews. He realized that we could help them fight stress and could help them with the right approaches. Guruji not only encouraged him to go ahead, but also directed him to the right people who could help him develop training modules and assist him, as well as provide for the money that was required to start up. There is another example of a person who wanted to conduct training for maidservants. He directed the person to the resources which could help him in arranging mock sessions and other preparations. Interestingly, he was even linked up with Karan, the earlier person, who was doing something similar.'

> Step three towards instigating people towards extraordinary visions: Play the role of a facilitator. Connect the unconnected.

Open Source leadership organizations are called so because they are truly open, including in those areas where conventional wisdom dictates certain information to be kept strictly under wraps. Framing of the organizational vision is one such area, which even liberal organizations kept reserved for their CEOs. However, Open Source leadership attacks this same space and exposes it to the whole organization. These New Age organizations constantly strive to ensure that every team member is as much a part of a shared vision as they are of its implementation, through concurrent inputs of different agendas, approaches and priorities. In Open Source leadership, organizational vision indeed emerges out of every nook and corner.

6

Scratching on a White Wall
Open Source Leadership Makes the Corporate Rule Book Redundant

---

In this section:
- How Semler got his employees out of the 'boarding school'
- Why we work more when we are playing and play more when we are working
- How your selfish streak can save Open Source leadership from breaking down

---

How Semler got his employees out of the 'boarding school'

Brazilian businessman Ricardo Semler's favourite questions start with a 'why', writes Dominique Haijtema, a journalist. 'Why should employees feel compelled to read their emails on Sunday evening, but cannot go to the movies on Monday afternoon? Why should they take work home, but cannot bring their kids to the office? Why should they have to sit for hours in traffic getting to office, while they could have utilized that time working out of home?' Semler questions every organizational principle that he sees around, because he thinks it stinks of hypocrisy.

'Companies say something but do exactly the opposite. They tell their employees they are all part of one big, happy family. However, they make it a point to frisk their workers on the way home. They penalize employees if they arrive ten minutes late and audit petty cash accounts of someone who has been with the company for two decades. What family searches its members for silverware as they leave the dinner table?' Semler wonders in his best-selling book, *Maverick*.

Semler refers to this as 'boarding school syndrome', where most companies treat their people like schoolchildren. They insist on telling them where they have to be at what time, what they need to be doing, how they need to dress, whom they should talk to, and so on. The presumption is that they would not do the right thing, unless told to do so—or worse, they would not do anything unless supervised.

Semler worries that if people are treated like immature wards, they would increasingly behave like that. They would never think for themselves, try new things, or take chances.

Instead, he argued, people were naturally capable of self-direction and self-control, if they were treated as mature adults. They need not be driven with sticks, since even children could be trusted to do the right thing, given the right environment, he concluded.

Semler got a practical taste of things when he worked for his father's company, originally called Semler & Company, then a shipbuilding supplier in São Paulo. Semler's ideas directly clashed with his father's, who supported a traditional autocratic style of management laced with rules and laws of all kinds. 'How can I spend the rest of my life doing this? How can I stomach years of babysitting people to make sure they clock in on time? Why is this worth doing?' he raised his voice.

His father reassured himself that his son would grow out of this phase soon. The reality dawned upon Semler Sr only after he threatened to leave the company. Rather than see this happen, he resigned the CEO position and vested majority ownership to his son in 1980, when Semler was merely twenty-one years old.

That's when Semler started his revolutionary journey. His first challenge was to make sure that all employees were treated like responsible adults rather than like schoolchildren. He scrapped all those rules that restricted employees.

Semco soon had no set work hours, assigned offices or desks and dress codes. All employee manuals, rules and even the human resources department were abolished. People were allowed to work when they felt like and could go home when they wanted. They could decide when to take their holidays and how much vacation they needed. They could even choose how much they would be compensated.

In other words, Semco started to treat their employees like adults. And they started to expect them to behave like adults. Ultimately, the only focus was on performance. As long as people were performing, no questions were asked. An employee who spent two days a week at the beach but still produced real value for customers and co-workers was considered a better employee than one who worked twelve hour days but created little value. If an employee made mistakes, he was expected to take the blame, rather than pass the buck. Everyone was expected to be responsible—to themselves and to the organization.

However, conventional organizational wisdom says this could be a sure recipe for disaster. If employees were let free to set their own hours, any rational individual would come in as late as possible, and leave as early as possible, utilizing office hours for his own self-serving purposes. And, if employees were given a choice whether to attend meetings or not, they would abscond from important ones to pursue trivial matters.

Surprisingly, in Semco 'No Rules' did not mean chaos, instead added flexibility that came along with a clearly marked responsibility towards the system. 'No Rules' meant staying away from the lure of an 'only way' to open up people's minds to several new ones—that could enable them to be agile, change directions, and to adopt what was good and give up what was not. Semler cites the example of how the freedom to choose one's own working hours, thought to be a disastrous idea by many inside Semco itself, helped employees solve the problem of time wastage in the paralysing traffic jams of São Paulo. It was also thought that flexible scheduling would never work in an assembly-line production scenario. However, again, employees used their freedom not to be misused but to develop a new set of accountabilities. They reorganized themselves voluntarily so that certain groups would be at the factory at the same time. The new-found flexibility was used to suit personal priorities. Nevertheless, professional ones were not ignored. Work continued undeterred.

However, Lawrence M. Fisher, a contributing editor to *strategy+business*, in his article 'Ricardo Semler Won't Take Control', offers a word of caution. He writes that though a 'No Rules' system is definitely practical, organizations should still resist the impulse to transform overnight. In one of his interviews, João Vendramin Neto, who oversaw Semco's manufacturing, compared this hurried eagerness to reform to a watermelon truck with its tailgate open—all of them would roll out, and there would be utter confusion.

At the same time, a half-hearted or piecemeal approach again would not help, suggests Fisher. The No Rules policy has to be implemented in full for it to work, one step at a time, from simpler measures to more complex ones, giving time for people to adapt themselves to the new environment, quite different from the conventional ones that they are used to. Semco started out with eliminating smaller rules like fixed time and dress codes, but once employees got the hang of it, they went on to more complex ones like setting their own salaries and defining their own goals. The rolling out of the entire process took almost five years, with plenty of bumps and false starts, but Semco was ultimately a true 'No Rules' system.

However, Semco does not exist in Utopia. It is not altruism that governs it, but pure business logic. Semler writes that this model enabled Semco to survive through the gyrations of Brazil's tortured politics and twisted economy—a nation which has swung from right-wing dictators to left-wing populists, and an economy that has spun from rapid growth to deep recession. Brazilian banks have failed and countless companies have collapsed, but Semco lives on—to be a US$160 million corporation, up from US$4 million when Semler joined the family business almost three decades ago, often growing between 30 and 40 per cent a year.

Why we work more when we are playing and play more when we are working

'Why would a No Rules system work? It should never work,' exclaims the CEO of a large multinational corporation as we narrated the Semco experiment to him. However, it works. Not once in a while, but all the time.

In *Maverick*, Semler suggests that in any environment it is merely 2 to 3 per cent of people who take advantage of the employer's trust. But the management subjects the majority of 97 to 98 per cent equally to a daily ritual of humiliation, assuming that this gives them a better control over the proceedings. However, if we were to sit down and analyse how much control these tight-fisted rules bring in, we would discover that it is nothing much to write home about. Can strict timings make sure that productivity is improving, or can dress codes ensure more satisfied customers? The chances are high that they have no impact at all. 'In fact, it would probably be better to have a few cases of cheating once in a while than to condemn everyone to a system based on mistrust because most responsible adults know how to make sure that the systems that they are accountable for are working smoothly, and ensure trivial issues like how to dress correctly for occasions.' So, in short, just as rules do not ensure a greater outcome, the absence of them does not deny any greater outcome.

Management controls are the greatest bane of a traditional system, where they rely on stringent rules to keep a check. However, Open Source leadership realizes that rules do not serve any specific purpose. They just send out the wrong message to people that they do not have the capacity to control themselves. As this message is reiterated, they increasingly act in ways that are consistent with it. But when people are considered as mature adults, they would be more responsible towards themselves as well as towards the system. Hence, Open Source leadership embraces a No Rules system enthusiastically.

'We try to run Biocon with the minimum amount of rules possible', says Murli Krishnan, the president of Group Finance. 'Compared to some of the software companies, this might not seem to be very surprising. But we need to understand that manufacturing units are run in a very different fashion. Here rules are of primary importance, so that production can go on without any disruption. Still, we do not monitor the timing of people at all. People come, they finish at whatever time and they leave. Many of them come early in the morning and leave earlier. Some others come in late and stay late.

'This flexibility has given us some unexpected advantages. Better than any mechanical system, which fixes and enforces rule that are far away from ground realities, people in a flexible system are able to use their own human logic to adjust their timings to bring in the maximum amount of productivity. For some, this means beating the ruthless Bangalore traffic, while for some others it means being flexible according to their clients' needs. While for still others, for example ladies, it means being in office sans worries about their kids because they can adjust their timing in such a way that they could send their kids to school and return back in time. It is no longer just punching in the requisite number of hours that matters, but much more than that.'

Haresh Chawla says they run Network18 in a similar fashion, which he refers to as the 'spirit of a start-up'—an environment characterized by no strict rules or agenda. He says if an outsider were to visit their office on any given day, he would see more of chaos than a stiff and formal corporate environment. This thriving in an environment of less rules gives them the required agility to survive and thrive in a tough market. According to him, more rules, though it could give an illusion of control, could actually slow them down and act as a recipe for absolute disaster. The sprit of a start-up culture releases Network18 employees out of their boarding school syndrome. People are perceived and treated as adults—they are expected to judge and take charge of every opportunity without being told to do so.

The No Rules system works in a completely different manner from an 'All Rules' system. The latter works on the basic concept of control—affecting others to get the outcome that an organization expects by either coercing them with threats or inducing them with payments or rewards. Joseph S. Nye Jr from the Harvard Kennedy School of Government refers to this as 'hard power'. Unfortunately, in the No Rules system there is little hard power, which in reality could lead to chaos, unless balanced by some other factor. Semler writes that though we are conventionally led to believe that the balancing factor has to come vertically—pushed down from the top—in the absence of which, it could emerge from another surprising arena, horizontally, from the peers through the soft pressure that they exert. Peer pressure takes the place of rule-based controls in influencing others and in keeping the system in order.

Semco has an appropriate example to demonstrate this soft pressure of employees setting their own compensation. In normal cases, such freedom could have led to the exploitation of the system. However, in the case of Semco, the peer pressure stepped in at the right moment as the balancing factor. The system was in fact carefully designed to be so. First, this exercise was preceded by a good amount of homework—a series of detailed analysis, which benchmarked pay levels across multiple positions in different companies. The results of this benchmarking exercise were published across the company, so that employees had a reference point to look up to before they could decide what they were worth.

Secondly, freedom was given not only to define one's own salaries, but also to identify those people whom you preferred to work with—people who, you thought, could add value to your project. So, if an employee went ahead and defined his salary higher than all the peers, but could not justify it in terms of performance, he simply got under tremendous pressure. No one would want to work with him, or no team would want to take on the high expenses that the person brought with him to the team.

This freedom strategy of Semco resonates well with a fable. A king who once faced the dilemma of dividing his kingdom equally between his two quarrelling sons, let one of them divide it, while the other one had the right to choose his half first. The strategy of both parties having a say in the matter ensured the much elusive balance of equity and justice. 'From a distance it can sound like a workers' paradise,' writes Semler, 'but the system is pretty unforgiving, because if you put your salary too high, and people don't put you on the list as someone they need for the next six months, you are in more trouble than you would be at General Motors.'

Step one to freedom: Establish a sound system of checks and balances. Where rules do not come top-down but from peer pressure.

'Team coordination is of critical importance in a manufacturing environment. However, allowing people to choose their own timings has not affected our productivity in any manner,' says Murli Krishnan. 'It is interesting to see how our people work out a fine balance between organizational commitments and personal conveniences as they finalize on the production plans. All people would not get their way all the time, because team coordination is of primary importance. People are mature and they understand this. At times, you do get things your way, but you appreciate the fact that someone else sacrificed his personal priorities so that you could have yours. You could come in late because some other person stepped in to back you up, or the entire team decided to delay some meeting. However, the team also expects you to reciprocate, the next time around, even if that means a sacrifice from your side. Else, you are an odd man out. So, though there is enormous amount of freedom, this system works well because of personal understanding, maturity and reciprocity.'

'You could do whatever you pleased in the dressing room, as long as you were playing well and supporting each other well,' says Zach from the Indian cricket team. 'Because we were playing fabulously well, people outside thought there was something magical about the Indian dressing room. Some thought we were being given pep talks all the time by the captain while some others thought good tips on performance were doled out by our coach. Not so. In fact, the Indian dressing room at that point was marked by a complete no-rules system. There was nothing like we could not talk loud, or we had to focus on one thing. We were allowed to shout, we were allowed to sing and were allowed to do whatever we pleased. We were always playing pranks on each other, laughing and pulling each other's legs. Some people preferred sleeping, while some others played their music.

'At the same time that meant as a team we were supposed to fall into place the minute we stepped on to the field. If, someone failed to support someone else in the team, be it in bowling, batting or fielding, the pressure on that person would be high. Everyone wanted to play with people who could make them perform at higher levels. So, the individual task was in fact two-pronged: I had to play well, and at the same time I had to ensure that my teammates also played at their best potential. The second was as important as the first, whether it meant fielding in a new position or a star batsman playing a supporting role, because the situation demanded so. So, at times you could insist that you would play only at a certain position as a batsman. You could score a century in that position, but if all the rest of the team failed miserably, because you were selfish about your performance, fingers were immediately pointed towards you. You could never get away saying that you played well; you had to ensure that you were good with all players in order to truly secure your position in the team.'

> Step two to freedom: Give freedom in such a way that it gives opportunities to take some and give some. Reiterate collaboration and reciprocity between individuals.

Peer pressure as well as reciprocity works, not only in setting salaries, but also in most other cases where stringent rules are absent. For example, in the case of Semco, employees have the freedom to choose their own laptops, or their own hotels while travelling. But if one decided to stay in a five-star, while his colleagues stayed in a three-star, pressure was on him to justify it in terms of performance. As long as the person is performing excellently it does not matter whether he came in late or he played golf all morning. In the No Rules system, peer pressure rules. The writing on the wall is clear—you better be as good as the salary, the laptop or the hotel you choose, else be prepared to stand out like a sore thumb.

Swamy Pragyapath says that Art of Living follows the same No Rules culture. The system gives them freedom to decide their own path. No one would ever chastise you because you were not moving in a given path.

'There are no dos and don'ts here. Everybody recognizes that every other person is at a certain level of spiritual growth—like in the sky, where every star has its own position. We can never say that this star is higher or another one is lower. Everyone has a position here.

'At times, some new projects claim more than the resources that were allocated for it. That could lead to differences of opinion because more to one project means less to another one. However, people handle this with maturity. As long as the project is justifying the resources, these differences of opinions would not come out in the open. They remain as undercurrents—at a personal level, but not at a systemic level. However, if resources are not justified, or if results are not visible, the pressure becomes real. People start asking questions. You have to be either ready with your answers or be ready to wind down.'

Step three to freedom: Give freedom to question everything.

Yet another balancing attribute that works extra hard to make sure that the No Rules Open Source leadership succeeds is transparency. Here nothing is hidden, everything is open for everybody else to see. In the case of Semco, salaries are made public, and so is all the company's financial information. A central website makes sure that everyone can communicate with everyone else and knows what is going on.

The transparency that pervades everything helps peer pressure work smoothly to a great extent. People know why someone is getting a promotion, why someone is claiming a higher salary or why someone is opting out of a meeting. It also helps them to keep a finger on the pulse of the company. They know exactly how much are the revenues, how much are the expenses, what is justified and what is not, organizationally as well as individually.

Step four to freedom: Keep everything transparent to everyone.

How your selfish streak can save Open Source leadership from breaking down

Ironically, another important factor that saves a No Rules Open Source leadership from breaking down into chaos is a streak of self-interest, something that our intuition tells us would perform an opposite role. Semler's idea is counter-intuitive: 'For a company to excel, employees must be reassured that their self-interest, not the company's, is their foremost priority.' He compares Semco to a free market, where people bring their talents and develop themselves by using the company as a platform. Here they are never forced to do anything that they do not want to, but are allowed to find a job that they like and are given a free hand to carry it out, sometimes even when it happens to be outside their area of expertise. At Semco, personal interest is given the highest priority. Everyone is responsible for their own career and training.

Semler draws on an interesting analogy with his young son in an interview to Stephen Moss of the *Guardian*. 'He'll say, "I don't want to eat this." So I say, "Don't eat it." People say, "My God, he will be undernourished and he will never eat vegetables." But it's not that simple. He'll eat fries for a week, but then he doesn't want to see fries for ten days. He is such a sophisticated piece of machinery; we don't come close to understanding what makes him up. The chances are that whatever design he came built in he also knows that if greens are good for him, he is going to want greens at some point. But the idea that I can get him to eat greens by force is a very stupid concept.'

Interestingly, this concept gets better as we analyse it in-depth. It starts from catering to the individual self-interest, nevertheless with an underlying strong thread of common organizational interest. There are three reasons for this. First, when people do everything out of their own interest and not because it is a job, they tend to be more passionate. Passion employs more enthusiasm and creative energy, which directly adds to productivity. Secondly, there tends to be more accountability, since they have chosen to do what they want to do. It is a personal choice more than any compulsion and hence people tend to do more justice to it. And thirdly, it also helps the company save much time and effort on those trivial issues that normally end up consuming most of management time. 'Boarding school' issues like when you come in, what you are called, what you are paid, whom you can talk to are no longer time consumers.

We draw on an interesting example which Semler once cited of the company cafeteria, which was a subject of endless complaints. The company's simple solution was to hand over the cafeteria management to a group of employees themselves. As they started catering what they wanted, the complaints stopped. Most importantly, as they went through the trouble themselves, employees learnt to empathize with the management. No Rules in Open Source leadership, though it smells of self-interest, eventually starts reflecting a larger organizational interest.

At Semco, people who are interested in taking on management roles are allowed to do so, irrespective of their experience. However, these managers would be anonymously evaluated every six months by their subordinates and would not be allowed to continue, if they did not measure up. Here again, personal interests eventually give way to organizational interests. As a person embraces a larger role than what he is eligible for, he would naturally stretch his capabilities to prove himself right as well as to be approved by his subordinates, in turn adding to the organizational productivity.

Voluntary attendance in meetings is yet another good example from Semco. Once meetings are announced, whoever is interested can show up, but can also leave the moment they are uninterested. This ensures that organizers of meetings have a huge responsibility to keep these meetings relevant to the right target audience. The pressure is also on the organizer to ensure that meetings remain short and interesting, which saves much organizational time and resources.

Vijaya Menon has an interesting illustration from her experience to demonstrate why personal freedom is not only good for individuals but also for the organization. In the airline industry, pickup and drop services for the crew members is almost a mandatory service. However, this has its own problems. Sometimes a whole bus would travel to drop a couple of individuals, while at other times the entire crew would wait endlessly for a pilot at his doorstep.

Air Deccan decided to loosen up this system. It was decided that the company would pay a fixed travel allowance rather than providing company pickup and drop services. That resulted in a quick turnaround in the attitudes of employees. Air hostesses who earlier refused, started sharing their taxis, and some even started opting for cheaper alternatives like autorickshaws. Vijaya suggests that this system even had a very positive impact on the overall punctuality of their staff. It improved dramatically, because they could no longer blame the company system for their delays. For the individual employees, it meant a freedom to choose their own mode of transport and even better saving opportunities, while for the organization it meant getting rid of an entire block of logistics and better accountabilities.

Zach complements, 'When a person is given freedom to choose than a choice being thrust upon him, better results are ensured. If a captain is deciding on everything from who would bat at which position and who would bowl, the onus is on the captain himself. It is also a tough task for one individual to handle—coordinating between the batting, fielding, bowling—all at the same time. He can miss out on a lot of details, which someone else is seeing. But, if a team is given the freedom to express their thoughts, individual players can gauge the situation and act accordingly. For example, sometimes as a bowler, I have the gut feeling that I am going to pick up wickets. In a flexible system, I would go up to my captain and ask for an extra over. I could convince him that though I have completed my pre-decided spell, I am confident of a breakthrough. I could also ask for a specific field which fits in my new over. It seems like it is in my interest that I bowl this extra over, but in reality, I am aware that someone has sacrificed his over for me, so I shall push myself extra hard to produce results, which is actually very good for the team.'

If checks and balances are properly in place, organizational interests need not be thrust upon team members/employees. Self-interests can automatically lead to these.

'But, we are also convinced that this balance would work only as long as there is a common interest,' revealed Semler once to a newspaper, pointing towards another important attribute that helps No Rules in Open Source leadership work. Interestingly, an automatic control system develops in an organization when people take an active concern in the daily affairs. When people are not only interested in their affairs, but also in the work that their peers are doing, they listen and they raise their voices when they need to. They do not keep quiet, but question all assumptions, whether they come from their peers or from their seniors. And that builds on to the pressure.

However, if people are indifferent about what is going on and are doing their nine-to-five blindly, life becomes difficult. That opens up the whole system for people to exploit and plunder. Every person knows that no one else cares about what he does, so he might as well make as much as he can. When a lot of people think the same way, the system is certain to be doomed. Open Source leadership could give all the freedom and ensure all the transparency, and still achieve nothing, if people are not involved.

'Yes,' comments Kiran Mazumdar Shaw. 'Freedom works when people are passionate not just about what they are doing, but in the overall well-being of the company. That is the time when each one of them can create a check and balance on the other. However, we cannot expect every person to be bothered about the overall well-being of the company from day one. So, we consciously try cultivating those values through different mechanisms, like making sure that there are more arenas for people to mingle around and interact, or by inculcating curiosity in things beyond their departments.'

Vijaya Menon agrees that the model works well only when all the people are aligned and are interested in each other. In normal companies, employees are taught to restrict themselves to their cubicles and to mind their own businesses. However, in Open Source leadership, people are forced to take an interest in each other—not only while working, but also while they are not.

People taking an active interest in the daily affairs of the organization help develop an automatic control system against any system exploitation.

'When you are given the freedom, your responsibility does not stop with bowling well. It extends—you have to make sure that your teammates are fielding with their lives for every run, that every over is economical, that every chance is taken up. It is not only up to the captain, but also up to each one of us,' says Zach.

Semler sums it up well. 'Freedom is no easy thing. It does not make life carefree—because it introduces difficult choices. It is much easier for people to give in to a familiar system in which they don't have to make any decisions.'

Opening the Floodgates with a Corkscrew

Open Source Leadership Breaks Down Organizational Silos by Building Permeability in the System

In this section:
- The interesting story of a CEO who moonlights as a baggage porter
- Why the most evolved organization structures should strive to be like the lowly amoeba
- How successful leaders force diversity in their organizations to produce the magical 'Medici Effect'
- Three steps to help you minimize the pain associated with fluidity and change

The interesting story of a CEO who moonlights as a baggage porter

Once in an interview to CNN, Tony Fernandes confided that he often gets pulled up by the new Malaysian airport security personnel mistaking him for a Bangladeshi immigrant. They think he has jumped off a B1 plane trying to be the next illegal immigrant. They cannot be blamed, because he is often conspicuously roaming around near the baggage counter in his baseball cap, open-neck shirt and jeans, at times even hefting suitcases on to the trolleys. However, we see the contrast whenever he strolls into the departure hall, where passengers approach him requesting photographs to be taken along with him. Because in reality Tony Fernandes happens to be the owner and CEO of

AirAsia, the first budget no-frills airline in Malaysia, which now has operations across the globe.

In his previous avatar, Tony Fernandes was the youngest ever managing director of Warner Music in Malaysia. When Time Warner Inc announced its merger with America Online Inc, Tony left to pursue his dream of starting a budget airline. However, this would not be so easy. As he approached the government for permissions, Dr Mahatir Muhammad, the wily Malaysian prime minister, advised him to buy an existing airline instead of starting from scratch. And that airline happened to be a heavily indebted subsidiary of the Malaysian government, which was losing money speedily. Tony mortgaged his home and sank all his savings to acquire the company, at a time when the whole aviation industry was sinking in the after-effects of the 11 September 2001 catastrophe. Yet, just one year after the takeover, his company, AirAsia, broke even and cleared off all its debts. Its initial public offering in 2004 was oversubscribed 130 per cent. AirAsia is now the pride of every Malaysian, and a role model for every airline in the industry.

Tony had almost no experience in the airline industry before he took over AirAsia. How did he manage to do this? In his interviews, Tony reveals an alarmingly simple answer. As he came in with no preconceptions, he could easily identify many of the problems in the industry, most of them caused by its rigid compartmentalization. The success of AirAsia is that, quite different from the other airlines, it is unstuffy, open and cheerful.

AirAsia has no watertight compartments. Everything is amorphous and permeable. It is characterized by an open culture, where people can move and are expected to move from one role to another without any hassles. Tony once commented about this. 'We put everyone together—marketing people, finance people, engineers, cabin crew, pilots—all in one office. It means effective communication. When people need help, we all go out, even if it is to carry bags. My secretary will go out and help clean the planes if we are running into a delay.'

Tony practises what he preaches. Every month he spends a day as a baggage handler; every two months, a day as cabin crew; every three months a day as a check-in clerk. 'It was weird when I first came to the airline, the pilots freaked out because they suddenly saw their CEO pushing the ladder. They stood to attention, they called me sir. They could not get over the fact that I have a cup of coffee with the guys who carry bags. I really believe this culture is behind our success.'

However, the fluidity and permeability of AirAsia culture does not end there. Compared to the normal plush airline offices, AirAsia stands out, because strangely they run theirs on a ramp, underneath Gate A6 at the Kuala Lumpur airport. This office has no walls, ensuring that there are minimal chances of building any internal empires—be it departmental or seniority-based empires. There are no dress codes. AirAsia's senior management rarely walk around in expensive suits, so that staff members do not feel intimidated about talking to them. They believe in casual dressing so much that even the chief pilot flies occasionally dressed in jeans.

In AirAsia, an Open Source leadership organization, they truly strive every day to break down all watertight compartments. It brings together people from different walks of life, from different professions and successfully melds them. There are pilots who started out as baggage handlers and stewards, while there are senior management personnel who carry bags and help in booking tickets.

AirAsia thrives in an industry where competition is cut-throat and survival is based on utmost fitness. Their unique culture contributes much to their success. People moving from one department to another and at times willingly immersing themselves into the bottom-most part of the organization helps them stay close to ground realities and hence make better decisions. Many CEOs and managers make mistakes in their decisions because they are sitting in offices away from the real action. AirAsia has a good example, an incident where the issue of belt holders came up, where it was thought to be unnecessarily adding to the costs. But crew members insisted that despite how much they cost, they were necessary. Tony was not initially convinced, but he learnt it first-hand when he spent his time as a baggage handler—almost breaking his back. The issue was settled immediately. 'I think it's fundamental to running my company, because unless you get down to the floor and see what is happening, you would not make effective decisions. I do it for two reasons. The first is to see what is going on and to make sure that I am making the right decisions. And the second thing is, I still want to discover these raw diamonds,' Tony comments.

Fluidity in the system also helps build camaraderie. Everyone is part of one family; they belong to the organization as a whole rather than to a specific department or a role, and this helps them empathize and understand each other. Everyone is flexible and supports each other—be it carrying bags, cleaning planes or managing passengers. At the same time, not being the prisoner of a specific role also helps to bring out the best in every person. 'You see someone who is carrying a bag suddenly flying a plane,' mentions Tony. That itself serves as a powerful motivator for everyone to do their very best, everyone to contribute towards the success of AirAsia.

Why the most evolved organization structures should strive to be like the lowly amoeba

Robert Putnam, a political scientist from Harvard, in his book *Making Democracy Work*, made a clear distinction between two kinds of social capital—bonding capital and bridging capital. Bonding, in the organizational context, occurs when you are socializing with people who are more or less like you: same department, same role and so on. Bridging is what you do when you make friends with people who are not like you, like people of another department or people who are above or below you in hierarchy. Bonding indeed is an important form of social capital, but for Open Source leadership, bridging capital is equally important.

In many organizations they assume that the two forms of social capitals are in some kind of a zero-sum relationship—that is if you have a lot of bonding, you cannot have bridging, and if bridging goes up, bonding must come down. Putnam argued that this assumption is both logically and factually false because people can not only have more friends with their own kind, but can also have friends from other departments and other roles. In fact, these two forms do strengthen each other, helping the organization possess not a few closely knit power centres, but departments that are overall gelling together.

Open Source leadership strengthens their bridging capital primarily by making their systems as flexible and as fluid as possible—so that people can freely move across functions and roles. As people move freely across the organization, they not only develop bridging capital, where they are friends with people across, but also develop competencies across functions, which can constrain the growth of a normal negative tendency found in most traditional closed organizations—a tendency to make oneself irreplaceable by not delegating and empowering.

As Pragyapath gave up the corporate ambitions of a student from IIT, and embraced the ideals of the Art of Living ashram, Sri Sri put him straight into the management of the ashram. Trained as an engineer, management was not one of his competencies— neither in terms of skill sets nor in terms of education. Pragyapath says that initially he misinterpreted the intention behind giving him, the junior member, such an important responsibility. He convinced himself that it was meant to be an opportunity to apply his world-class knowledge in engineering.

Pragyapath would go into the kitchen and would be surprised by the fact that the cook was not following an efficient process.

He would then take the cook aside to advise him. If the cook resisted, he would engage in a verbal fight. The cook was not the only one subjected to this. There were watchmen, cleaners, drivers, all of them senior to Pragyapath, but not able to reach the perfection that he wanted the ashram to reflect. As Pragyapath grew increasingly impatient with every deviation from perfection, he decided to complain.

However, Pragyapath says that meeting with Sri Sri changed his entire perspective about why a young engineer was given the responsibility of the management of the entire ashram, starting from his first day. He learnt that it was not because he would turn around the ashram to the precision of an engineering firm, but because Pragyapath would start reflecting the ideals of the ashram. Because that would be the easiest way for Pragyapath to immerse himself into the ashram ideals and understand how it worked. Pragyapath had misinterpreted the whole intention. He says, from the day he had that meeting with Sri Sri he started out on a new journey, in fact the same journey with a new purpose. He was no longer looking at what an IIT engineer can teach a cook, but at what a cook can teach an IIT engineer. Probably, the reason why Sri Sri decided to call him Pragyapath (his name before coming to the ashram was Prashanth), a combination of two Sanskrit words—'Pragya' meaning intelligence and 'Path' meaning feet.

Swami Pragyapath says the greatest learning that came from his unusual stint—where he was asked to do a job which he was neither trained for nor comfortable with—was that it helped him fight his initial insecurities and egos, to integrate into the system. 'When I first met guruji with my complaints about everyone who refused to fall in my scheme of things, he gave me a good hearing. And then he made me see the other side of the fence. He made me understand that I was not dealing with inanimate machines, but people in flesh and blood who had real feelings.' Continues Pragyapath, 'Till then, I had a feeling that I was put in charge of the management of the ashram because I was superior to the rest of them. But as I went back after my meeting, I started to deal with my own egos rather than trying to deal with others. The stint in managing the ashram, a task that I did not have competencies to do, helped me look inward, identify my insecurities, and then get back into a world where everyone was a leader, unlike earlier, where I perceived myself to be the sole leader.'

Vijaya Menon has a similar story to narrate about Air Deccan. 'I used to work for the Taj group of hotels, where I was handling the operations. When I first met Captain Gopinath, he assigned me to corporate communications, a function completely different from what I had done till then, and a function that I had no previous experience in. Initially, I thought that I was just an exception, but then I noticed that this was being followed as if it was a policy. We were actively encouraging people who were not from the airline industry to join us. Our thinking was clear. If people who were from the same industry kept coming in, we would keep doing everything the way it had always been done. It might work in the case of a company which was trying to maintain the status quo. However, we were not trying to do that. We were trying to go against the grain. And we constantly found that when people who were not used to the typical ways came in, they were hungry to learn new ways. And they remained flexible.'

Joseph Hoover, a sports journalist, narrates a similar story from the life of Vijay Pathwar, who was once the captain of the Karnataka state cricket team. Once when he was on a cricketing tour, he suffered a back injury and hence had to be dropped from the team. However, slowly he started regaining his form and started playing well in domestic cricket and Ranji trophy matches. One evening he got a call from Sourav Ganguly, the captain of the Indian cricket team, asking him whether he could bowl a good ten overs if he was selected back into the team. The interesting aspect was that Vijay was primarily a batsman not a bowler. But as Sourav alerted him about his selection into the team, his role was defined to be that of a bowler. Selecting Vijay back was Sourav's decision, and giving him a different role was again his decision. It was not decided as a half-hearted attempt, but because Sourav was confident that he would be able to deliver on his promises.

Step one to flexibility: Expose first-timers to responsibilities that they are not used to or trained in.

Giving first-timers roles and responsibilities different from what they are used to is one way of bringing about flexibility in watertight compartments. Yet there is another way through which Open Source leadership actively pursue this breaking down of walls—by making people flit through different roles and responsibilities, not just in the initial part, but throughout their career.

When it was founded more than half a century ago by Indian industrialists, the World Bank and the government of India, ICICI was envisioned as the first development bank for a newly independent nation. Today, ICICI Bank is India's largest privately owned bank with assets of nearly US$80 billion, as of March 2009, and has an expanding global reach. The group's story is not just one of growth, but of transformation: ICICI has evolved from a development bank to become a corporate and then a retail bank, and finally a universal bank, meeting the needs of a newly prosperous population. There is one person who evolved along with this transformation that created this great institution—Chanda Kochhar.

Starting out as a management trainee, Chanda Kochhar has traversed functions and roles. In the process of transforming a small bank into the largest private sector bank in the country within a decade of its inception, the various steps taken by Ms Kochhar also shaped the retail finance industry in India. A few of such path-breaking initiatives included launching electronic channels in banking, developing a large network of Direct Sales Agents, setting up of the Bancassurance model and a cross-sell model using various channels. In April 2001, she took over as executive director, heading the retail business in ICICI Bank and in May 2009, as the managing director and CEO of the bank, after having seen and experienced probably almost all the departments in ICICI from technology architecture to retail operations, from corporate communications to finance, and from project monitoring to sales.

Vikram Hazra narrates a similar experience. He strayed accidentally into Art of Living as he was researching for an article but decided to stay on, more than one-and-a-half decades back. When asked about his role in Art of Living, Vikram says that he has moved through almost all the roles possible—teacher, trainer, administrator and community servant—most of them not related to his background in media. According to Vikram, the best part about his job is the sheer amount of surprises that he is exposed to, as he moves smoothly from one role to another. He finds himself in almost the opposite ends of the spectrum every other day. He could be travelling to a place like icy cold Siberia (which he has done four times till now) or to some African village. He has also found himself in plush hotel rooms in New York just to fly out to some rural remote place in India, which does not even have access to running water. He recalls incidents where he has dined with some of the biggest corporate honchos as part of his corporate training programme, while the evenings were spent at the ashram helping in chores.

'It is very easy for me to say that I love being here. It is so peaceful. I would just stay over here for the rest of my life, perform the same role, meditate, do my yoga and get my Ayurvedic massage. But it would never work like that. The minute you think you are settling down, there is a crisis out there, and we just have to go out and mop it up. For example, I spent about five years travelling in the North-east to some of the villages. There would be no electricity. And to make a long-distance call I had to walk for miles. But the minute I was settling down into that life, I was called back to handle another task,' says Vikram. At the same time, Vikram, like Vijaya Menon, reiterates the fact that this passage through different roles is not an exception in Art of Living, but rather a norm.

Step two to flexibility: Make people flit through different roles and responsibilities, not just in the initial part, but throughout their careers.

Vikram suggests that this rotation of roles helps an organization like Art of Living—which is without any hierarchical levels—to function smoothly. 'When there are no hierarchies, two things could happen. Either you are reporting to no one or you are reporting to everyone. If the first case happens, it could be disastrous to the organization, because there would be no accountabilities at all. Everyone would shirk and no one would work. However, if the second scenario happens—where everyone reports to everyone else, where a person is accountable not to just one boss, but to the whole organization, it is great.

'The role rotation system helps the case because it helps break down all our egos. People who constantly nag other people about their jobs suddenly discover the difficulties and learn to empathize. It also helps create a close camaraderie between people from across departments.

'But do not think that this kind of a system is easily manageable—where rigid accountabilities can coexist along with flexible roles,' Vikram adds a caveat. It works in Art of Living because the role rotation system is backed up by a lot of faithfulness to the entire system rather than to individuals. Over here, we know that we are aiming for a bigger goal. Hence, all of us are ready to roll up our sleeves, when we are needed to, irrespective of whether we like it or not, whether we have the competency or not. But such a system might not work if people are attached to specific departments, or to their managers. Organizationally, the success of such a system requires a higher level of maturity. For example, though we have several problems between people, typical of any human community, the moment a consensus is reached on an organizational issue, these same people get together and work together, forgetting all their differences. Because ultimately they want the system to win, even if that means individually they lose out.'

Vikram says Art of Living is able to successfully implement their role rotation philosophy even in their new branches across the world. 'Most of the time, new branches come up when someone in a distant country feels that Art of Living is relevant for their society. The first step towards this is the constitution of an Art of Living Board for that country, which most of the times comprises some prominent people from that place. Then they would recruit an initial set of volunteers who can serve as teachers and organizers. However, most of the times, the same board members would also serve as volunteers in teaching and coordination. They shift through roles easily—they formulate the policies relevant for that country, arrange for locations where the classes could be held, clean up the premises as well as conduct the classes.'

'Even though I have worked for one institution throughout my career, I feel that I worked for several companies,' says Chanda Kochhar. 'What has been really defining for me in this is the fact that I have run many new and varied businesses for this organization. This has helped me develop a certain amount of detachment to any specific role. I am no longer attached to a task or a function. I can just pack my bags and leave—even at short notice, from an established department to a new one. For example, at some point of time, I was running the corporate side of the bank and was handling almost 50 per cent of its profits and assets and business. During that time consumer credit was at its infancy, almost accounting for less than 1 per cent of the bank's business. When my CEO asked me to take over the consumer credit business, I asked, "Why should I move from handling 50 per cent of the bank to handling 1 per cent of the bank?" I clearly remember him answering: "Because I want you to make this business more than 50 per cent of the bank." Ultimately, we made his prediction come true, where the newly formed department emerged as one of the largest, because I was willing to be flexible, at a time when I could have chosen to remain in my comfort zone.

'I remember this incident when we started up commercial banking,' continues Chanda. 'I was the first person in the team and I had to create the team. The only thing we had was one big hall and I was sitting there along with my team of thirty people. During that time, one of my earlier clients came to meet up with me, since something was still pending from that assignment. Previously, the client had met me in my posh office where I was doing large infrastructure financing. To his sheer amazement, I was now sitting amongst thirty tables and chairs. For a moment, he presumed that I had been demoted.

'But that is the way it is when things are flexible. You cannot sit in your glasshouse, but have to be in the midst of your people, living hand to mouth in terms of resources, and stretching yourself completely. For example, because we lacked commercial bank experience, we did not have pay-in slip books or chequebooks. So, I would sit along with my team and even design those. Experiences like these have helped me evolve as a person, and acquire the capability to see the bank from different angles. It has also given me the flexibility and an entrepreneurial capability to start from scratch, setting up the business and taking it up to a scale.'

Step three to flexibility: Make sure even the leadership goes through the fluid path.

Anuj Bhargava, a general manager at ICICI Bank, has been working for more than ten years. He is currently associated with Chanda as her executive assistant. He says he opted to work for Chanda, in an executive assistant position that was exclusively created for him, rather than being slotted in an existing one. According to him, a great advantage for anyone who works in ICICI Bank is the fact that it was earlier a development institution which later merged into the bank. This process created several subsidiaries and initiated several new businesses—in personal finance, infrastructural finance, insurance, leasing, compliance, etc. And that gives people the opportunity to move from one role to another freely, almost creating a feeling that one is working in ten different companies in several different roles, and not being confined to one for life.

Umesh is one of the senior members of Art of Living, having come to the ashram in 1996, when there were hardly ten people. During the last one decade, he has fulfilled the roles of administrator and coordinator, has looked into social advancement and has taught meditation. However, the most surprising fact is that for the last three years he is a full-time driver for Sri Sri Ravi Shankar. For conventional minds, this could seem like a downgrade—having started in the ashram at a much higher position than what he is occupying now. But he has an interesting perspective about this. He says that in open environments like Art of Living, people grow and are enriched from every situation, though for an outsider, this might seem odd. 'There is no apparent contradiction in this,' he says with a smile. 'Just like the modern Blackberry that I carry in the pouch that I clip on to my traditional dhoti. It takes an open mind to understand this.'

'Our world has become more flat than it ever used to be. With information and communication technologies like the mobile phones and the Internet, it is very easy for us to sit in Bangalore and do business for America,' says Vikram Hazra. 'At the same time, ironically, in this global village the distances between people have just widened more than ever before. Every organization smells of silos. One hand does not know what the other hand is doing. Employees who belong to one department are not supposed to be anywhere near the others. Or, people in the same room do not know each other except through their email addresses. So, it is one challenge to make this world a global village, but quite another challenge to make it into a global family.'

'That is the biggest advantage of this fluidity in our organization.' Swami Pragyapath takes it forward from the point where Vikram left off. 'In such a kind of system people know that they never settle down into a cosy nook. Today you might be here, but tomorrow you could be anywhere. That itself breaks down barriers between people. That itself is an incentive for people to go up to strangers and talk to them. And that builds the camaraderie. There are no strangers here, because everyone has worked with everyone else, or would in some time. So, the whole organization starts behaving like a family. We sit together, share our challenges and build consensus. Sometimes it works, while sometimes it does not. But people continue to be members of the same family.'

Step four to flexibility: Constantly unsettle people. Never let them settle down.

Anuj Bhargava comments that fluidity, though it seems to be unsettling for individuals, can be extremely beneficial. His primary example is that of Chanda, his boss, whom he considers as the one person who has taken advantage of this. Fluidity has helped her not only gain a good overview of the bank, but also to be flexible and agile—to adapt to situations quickly and easily. He gives an example of the time when Chanda moved to the 'control' function, something which she was new to. There were specialists who had been working in that function for several years—some of them decades even. But, Chanda hit the road running. She was not only able to grasp the basics, ask the right questions, engage them, but also was able to take it to the next level.

'In any business there are lot of contradictions and conflicts—of personalities, businesses, structures. So too in our business. It is a big challenge to hold all of that together. Chanda's wide array of experience helps her to be the glue that holds ICICI Bank together,' suggests Anuj. 'Chanda is able to do that because she has built a relationship with everyone—not through exercise of her power, but by working along with them and understanding them.'

Chanda has a point to add on this, 'Typically in any organization everyone knows the CEO, but the CEO does not know anyone other than the key members of his organization. I think my biggest advantage is that I have worked with almost everybody in the organization. I understand them and their predicaments—whether they have come from state-owned banks or other private sector corporations, whether they belong to corporate finance or retail banking. And that has two advantages. First, even when I am in a senior role, people still know that I am approachable. They have had some kind of direct working relationship with me. And second, it is much easier for me to understand and analyse their competencies, whenever we are undertaking mission-critical projects. It becomes easy for us to draw and hold together winning teams.'

Fluidity and flexibility will be with you on a long haul.

How successful leaders force diversity in their organizations to produce the Magical 'Medici Effect'

In Open Source leadership as well as in traditional closed ones, people come from a variety of backgrounds. Their culture, upbringing, interests, talents, education and everything else tend to be diverse and distinct. However, the similarities end right there. There are distinct differences between the ways Open Source leadership treats this diversity from their traditional cousins.

Traditional closed leadership treats the whole organization as one large 'melting pot'. Anyone who enters is automatically thrown into this 'pot' where a process of assimilation takes place. All the distinctiveness that one brings into it are blended together or melted to reflect what the organization wants. During this process, the interests of each individual are extinguished to bring out a completely new mixture. In the case of Open Source leadership, there are no melting pots, but only 'salad bowls'. Here, every individual, group and their interests are treated as separate and distinct. Each one of these form an essential part in making up the whole. Everyone is considered to be one of the tastes or ingredients that contribute in forming the whole; and hence retain their original characteristics. For example, in Zappos, they enable people to celebrate their individualities by allowing them to decorate their own cubicles, in whichever crazy way they want these to be. Even in their calls with customers, they do not have any specific scripts to follow—each executive is allowed to come up with his own script. 'We embrace diversity of individualities, personalities and creativities, even at the risk of being perceived as a little inconsistent and weird,' suggests Tony.

In Open Source leadership salad bowls, even as the organization remains fluid and amorphous, there is still no pressure to assimilate to the point of losing your distinctiveness. The biggest advantage of a salad bowl over a melting pot is interestingly called 'the Medici Effect', a term suggested by Frans Johansson in his best-selling book by the same name.

> In Open Source leadership, there are no melting pots, but only salad bowls. Here, every individual, group and their interests are treated as separate and distinct.

Johansson named the 'Medici Effect', after the fifteenth-century banking family from Florence that broke down traditional barriers separating disciplines and cultures to ignite the Renaissance in Europe. Johansson's idea is simple. He writes that the diversity and distinctiveness in a salad bowl kind of organization helps in developing an 'Intersection'—a place where myriad ideas and interests meet and collide, ultimately igniting an explosion of extraordinary new innovations. He says that when people with diverse interests and talents come together, they end up inspiring each other in combining existing concepts into a large number of extraordinary new ideas.

'As people from industries other than airlines joined Air Deccan a burst of new innovative ideas happened,' reiterates Vijaya Menon. 'These people did not have a baggage of experience in the airlines industry. So they started inter-acting with each other, in formal meetings, in casual chit-chats, in conference rooms, around the water cooler. They started thinking about airline problems in non-airline ways. Some brought in their experience from the hotel industry, someone else from direct marketing, while someone else from selling soaps. Suddenly nothing was sacrosanct.'

Step one to the salad bowl approach: Let people come without any baggage. And then ask them to share baggage.

'Innovations started happening at Air Deccan as if by magic. For example, the way tickets were being sold. Travel agents were the primary route until then. But agents came with a mindset. They required merchandise. They considered hefty commissions as their right. These were challenges for a low-cost airline. So, we came up with an Internet model. And we came up with an incentive system that would force people to go off travel agents—that if they booked tickets through the Internet they would get great bargain deals. Then there were these other innovations, unheard of in the airline industry, but drawn from other industries like telecommunications, FMCG (fast-moving consumer goods), etc. We started selling our tickets through mobile outlets, post offices, petrol bunks. With the existing resources, we started earning more money. And through our unconventional strategies driven by these people who had absolutely no clue about airlines earlier we started a revolution,' says Vijaya.

Tony suggests that when people at Zappos are encouraged to express themselves in smaller and trivial things, two advantages emerge. Firstly, it engages them, because people are celebrating their own unique personalities. Secondly, they get comfortable with the fact that they need not follow the conventional path. It encourages them to think out-of-the-box when it comes to issues that are more serious. 'So, when they see people decorating their cubes, or some other crazy idea like having a parade to the office, and that we are supporting them in that, they feel more comfortable. It ends up being a win-win for everyone: Employees are happier at work, and the company as a whole becomes more innovative.

Chanda Kochhar has her own 'Medici Effect' story to tell. She says that they knew ICICI Bank could not afford to do things in the same old conventional ways, if they wanted to achieve a global scale. 'If we had to grow to handle 40 million customers, we had to really stick our necks out and learn. One way was to get people from other domains inside the bank so that we could learn from their diverse experience. Another way was to just go out and learn. So, we just went out: to manufacturing companies to see how they managed their production process, to automobile companies to learn how an assembly line is run, to airlines to learn how they handled their customer service and to retailers to learn how to manage operations. We even went to logistics companies to learn how to push paper faster, cut bureaucracies. And as we did these our minds suddenly opened up. Very soon, we started innovating products, processes and systems that could help us issue 10,000 credit cards a day or open 10,000 accounts a day. We went from best practices in banking to next practices.'

Johansson has an explanation for why this flurry of innovations happens when people are fluidly moving across functions. He refers to it as low associative barriers. Typically, whenever there is a problem, our minds unravel a chain of associations, each one connecting to every other. These chains of associations tend to be clustered around domains related to our own experience, leading to a high barrier for association to anything beyond. So, when a ticketing problem has to be solved by an airline professional, he would always recall how the problem had been handled in the past, or how others in similar situations solved it, coming out with common and predictable solutions.

However, when people start drawing from the experiences of a wide variety of individuals, domains and functions, the barriers to association break down—where people are able to easily connect different concepts across fields. There would be chains of associations taking irregular paths outside of a specialized field, rather than predictable ones inside. So here we have companies like ICICI Bank, which when trapped in a constraint of underutilized ATMs in rural areas, learn from the experience of village vegetable vendors to innovate mobile ATMs. Here, mobile ATMs go around in vans through standard routes servicing villagers. Indeed, a fitting ode to the Medici family.

Step two to the salad bowl approach: Encourage people to relate familiar problems to unfamiliar and unrelated sources.

However, the advantages of a salad bowl approach in Open Source leadership do not end there. In recently published research, authors Katherine Phillips, Margaret Neale and Katie Liljenquist found that members of a group were more likely to voice unique perspectives and critically review task-relevant information when there was more social diversity present rather than when there was not. Surprisingly, this was true even when the people who were 'diverse' did not express any unique perspectives themselves—they did not necessarily ask tougher questions, possess novel information or doggedly maintain a conflicting point of view. The mere presence of this diversity itself made people with independent points of view more willing to voice out and others more willing to consider those perspectives in a way that benefited the group.

The research also suggested that a salad bowl approach not only brought out a flurry of new ideas, but also helped in better execution compared to a melting pot. The authors had a simple logic about this. When people who were different agreed with one or more of the ideas, this agreement itself put pressure on the propounders to focus more keenly on success. They essentially wanted to do justice to the trust expressed by the other members and hence tried harder than the members in a melting pot.

> People thought harder and worked harder when they were distinct members of a salad bowl and did not melt in the pot.

Three steps to help you minimize the pain associated with fluidity and change

Talking about fluidity in an organization is one thing, but pulling it off successfully amidst complexities is a different task altogether. Because at the end of the day, whether in open or traditional closed leaderships, organizations are dealing with people who are almost always afraid of changes, and more so of frequent ones. All of us like to settle down into the comforts of a known place. But organizational fluidity talks about exactly the opposite. So, how does Open Source leadership work on overcoming these resistances?

Tony Fernandes of AirAsia thinks that it is all about setting the right example. There are definitely many people who would like to settle down the conventional way—doing one job for a lifetime and being in the comfort and security of that role. 'Yet, even for them, it becomes very hard when they see the CEO doing it. Then they have to do it,' he says.

When asked about this, Vikram Hazra pointed out to two young chaps who were sitting out there in the ashram lawn surrounded by a few people. They were sorting out issues regarding room allocation for about 2,000 people who had registered for the advanced meditation course at the Art of Living. He suggested that though this rigmarole would go on till the wee hours of the night, and though they had to don the mantle of teachers for this course early in the morning, they would still be dedicated. 'What keeps them there is the example set by guruji himself,' says Vikram. 'I think the motivation for all of us is that if we don't do it, guruji would do it himself. That is a bit of a scary thought.'

Vijaya Menon agrees with this. She says her role model was right in front of her eyes every day—in the form of Captain Gopinath, who left the army in 1979 and ventured into farming, in a barren desert land, principally occupied by snakes and scorpions. He lived there in a tent, which he pitched himself, taking care of the land along with a young boy, who served as an assistant, a dog and his motorcycle. He went on to rear silk worms; developed indigenous techniques of eco-friendly farming that later won him the Rolex International Award for Enterprise. He later opened a consultancy and even wrote scientific papers on the subject. His adventures did not stop there. He took over an Enfield brand motorcycle agency in Hassan, a district in Karnataka, turned it around, played the role of an event manager for some time, conducted the first beauty contest in Hassan, later ventured into stockbroking, ran a restaurant, and even gave politics a shot by standing for elections before setting up Air Deccan. 'Can there be a better example for the fact that every task can be enriching, no matter big or small, if you take to it in the right manner?' questions Vijaya.

Step one to breaking the inertia: Set an example. Make your people ask 'What would my leader do?'

'Changes can become easier, if you let it be,' says Chanda Kochhar. 'Many a time, change seems to be difficult because there are lot of unknown elements to it. You don't know what is in store for you. You don't know whether you can cope up with it or not. You don't know how the people over there would react to you. There are a thousand questions running in your mind, leading to a thousand insecurities. One way this can become easier is if you know the people around in the place where you are venturing into. The mere assurance that they are there to help you win rather than pull you down can settle you down.

'I remember the time when ICICI Bank took over Bank of Madura. Bank of Madura was much smaller compared to ICICI and there was a lot of insecurity all around. So we ensured that there was a mix of people in every branch—from ICICI Bank as well as from Bank of Madura. That ensured that people were talking to each other and understanding each other. Another incident that I remember is my visit to Pune, incidentally on the day the acquisition was announced. We decided that we would visit Bank of Madura branches even before the ICICI ones. And as we entered the branch, I handed over a bouquet to the manager and welcomed him to the ICICI Bank family. Normally, a director would be greeted like that. But we decided to break the mould. And that served as a powerful metaphor for what we were trying to express—that we are one family now. That simple act won the entire Bank of Madura over.'

> Step two to breaking the inertia: Consciously construct smaller comfort spaces for your people to ease their progress towards larger and more painful changes.

'At the same time, there are other larger challenges also with a fluid structure, especially from an organizational context,' suggests Chanda Kochhar, 'the main one being the smooth functioning of the organization itself. So, the role rotation and free movement across functions would have to be done as a process rather than as a random act. You have to ensure that while you shift, you do not disrupt what is already going on. You allow what is going on to continue, additionally build in new things and then gradually make sure that the two are gelling and people are feeling comfortable.

'Fluidity is a very delicate process. You have to have the balance of neither overdoing it under nor under-doing it. If you overdo it, you will kill the existing momentum at the cost of something new. If you play it down it, you will just end up creating entities that are not talking to each other. So a lot of time has to be spent on ensuring that people are talking to each other, individuals and their insecurities are taken care of, even as roles are getting changed and teams are getting integrated. However, once you pull it off, that itself is the biggest joy.'

Step three to breaking the inertia: Fluidity is a delicate process. Handle it with care.

In Open Source leadership, they truly strive to break down all watertight compartments. They bring together people from different walks of life, not to create a melting pot, but to nurture a culture where they can move around from one role to another without any hassles. In Open Source leadership, everyone is part of one family; they belong to the organization as a whole, rather than to a specific department or a role—helping them empathize and understand each other. Everyone and everything is kept flexible and fluid. As people move freely across the organization, they develop competencies across functions, come up with newer and innovative ideas, and even execute them better.

Constant Cradling for Creating Rock Stars

Open Source Leadership Relies on a Culture of Coaching for Ensuring Better Integration and Performance

In this section:

- How Dav Whatmore used his 'Gospel of Coaching' to transform underdogs into winners
- Why our selfish individual interests should precede team interests, if you really want to win
- Why the best coach is a father figure
- Why things that are going wrong, if left so, can produce miraculous results

How Dav Whatmore used his 'Gospel of Coaching' to transform underdogs into winners

Surprisingly, Dav Whatmore emerged as a cricketing hero not when he played, but when he stopped playing. He retired from professional cricket in 1989, where his international career lasted under a year, to pursue a career in coaching. He coached the Sri Lankan national team in two separate spells; during the first one, they won the 1996 Cricket World Cup. In between those spells, he coached Lancashire, where they emerged victors in the National League in 1998 and 1999, and the NatWest Trophy in 1998. From 2003 to 2007, he coached Bangladesh, a team that had not won a match in several years. Under Dav, they captured their first Test match victory early in 2005. Later that year, Bangladesh shocked the cricketing world with a victory over the top-ranked team, Australia. During the 2007 World Cup, they again defeated a top-ranked South Africa, and then India, to reach the Super 8 stage.Late 2007, Dav took over as the director of the National Cricket Academy in Bangalore, terming it as an endeavour to create the next-generation cricketing stars so that people could remain glued to the game.

Dav, during his stint as a coach, turned underdogs into winning outfits. He effectively instilled a new optimism and discipline, especially in the case of Bangladesh, thereby initiating a comprehensive transformation from their 'defeatist attitude' towards a 'victorious approach'. His success has a lot to do with what he calls the 'gospel of coaching', in which he strives towards creating an atmosphere where the team management, captain and the board are all mutually encouraging and supportive of every individual player's growth.

Coaching is gaining popularity as a critical tool for organizational development and improved business results, even in some of the traditional closed organizations—whether the focus is on new employees or leaders, providing access and skill enhancement to certain groups, or accelerating the development of the best and brightest. However, what Dav calls 'a culture of coaching' is starkly different from this.

In traditional organizations, there is almost always a mechanical and direct focus on an alignment to a process or on business metrics—evaluation and reporting of results, retention, employee engagement scores, etc. But Open Source leadership views coaching or mentoring (though there are differences, in this chapter coaching and mentoring are used as interchangeable terms) as a direct way to nurture relationships and social capital; and indirectly as a way to enhance results, by relying on the improved bonding, rather than merely as a mechanical productivity enhancement tool. Here, coaching involves a relationship rooted in mutual respect and rapport rather than on organizational systems and processes.

In Open Source leadership, coaching is not a favour that is offered to employees to integrate them into the organizational culture, nor is it a perk that is doled out for their high performance, it is an integral part of the culture itself. Here, competencies need not be acquired from an outside entity but already exist inside the organization and are passed on. While in traditional closed organizations coaching is a specialized activity, involving specialist coaches, in Open Source leadership it is an open activity—here everyone coaches everyone else, they learn from and encourage one another.

In Open Source leadership, coaching is a relationship, not a process.

Rahul Dravid, a senior in the Indian cricket team, nicknamed 'The Wall' for his consistency and accuracy of technique, comments that it was this openness to mentor and be mentored that made all the difference to Sourav Ganguly's team. However, Rahul refuses to give credit to any one person or entity—be it the captain or the coach—for the creation of this winning team. 'It was a variety of factors. Most importantly, we had a good group of senior players who were all looking to take our game to the next level, whether it was Sachin, Laxman, Kumble, Srinath, Sourav or I. Quite early in our stints, we realized that we were not competing against each other, and we would not be able to sustain without the others' support. There naturally emerged a kind of mentoring network, where we started helping each other. We had our own strengths and understanding of the game. We shared that and helped the other person improve.

'We also created an atmosphere where new players could come in and give their best, without any sort of intimidation from the seniors. New players were free to interact with the seniors, learn from our experience, express themselves and work hard—in terms of confidence, fitness and techniques. So, we already had a core group of senior guys who were performing quite well and then when we had a few youngsters coming in to supplement and support that group, it became a pretty formidable combination.

'There was yet another dimension to this mentoring process,'Rahul continues. 'That was the support staff. We got a physiotherapist, a trainer and a good foreign coach. Along with them, we had a set of great team managers and selectors. These people added on to this mentoring network. People like John Wright, who was the coach at that point of time, helped in sustaining a good environment which allowed people to keep moving and working hard.'

Step one to coaching: Coaching is a culture, an environment.

'At the same time the open environment that automatically emerged ensured that no one was monopolizing the system for his superstardom. If anyone did, everyone would have lost faith in the system and it would have crumbled down. There would no longer be open sharing, because there would be insecurities all around. In our system no one was above the other—be it the players, the captain, the coach, the selectors or team management. This mutual understanding and confidence helped in minimizing insecurities, enabling people to give their best when they were supporting others. All these things added up. All of them made a difference, little by little.'

Step two to coaching: A coaching culture breaks down if anyone monopolizes it for his own superstardom.

Prof. Balram, director of IISc, adds to this point as he says that contrary to conventional wisdom, in a mentoring process, it is not only the student who gains but also the mentor. He says that whenever there is an active interaction in an open environment, the student gains from the experience and knowledge of the mentor, while the mentor is rejuvenated by the enthusiasm that his student brings along. Prof. Balram agrees that he himself has had many experiences, where the students brought fresh perspectives into an old research problem, because they were young, unbiased, read things which he did not, and experienced problems in newer ways.

'New ideas come in during this process from both sides. Many ideas are not of much use, some ideas are worth considering, and the remaining few ideas should be adopted. However, you would not get ideas to adopt unless you are willing to listen. You must get a lot of noise before you get some signal out of it. A good mentor listens to his student as much as he speaks,' says Prof. Balram.

Rahul Dravid agrees with this viewpoint that everyone learns in an open mentoring process. 'Yes, the juniors of course gained much, since we had much more international experience. But the truth is that we also did learn, because there was infusion of a new confidence. We were suddenly willing to experiment in unconventional ways. It was a great combination.'

> Step three to coaching: Mentoring is a two-way street. The mentor should be as willing to learn as the student.

Why our selfish individual interests should precede team interets, if you really want to win

There is yet another way the 'culture of coaching' differs from that of the traditional closed ones—its point of focus. Mentoring in traditional organizations is all about organizational goals, and how teams can be equipped towards those. The growth of individuals or their personal problems fade out in importance compared to organizational priorities. Hence, little attention is paid to those. However, Open Source leadership is firstly about individuals and only then about organizations.

'Coaching is not about an entire team, but about individuals. It is about individuals to see clearly what their strengths are and where they are lacking, and helping them set personal goals. When I took over Bangladesh national team, they were in bad shape. They had never won a Test match until then, but had suffered several defeats with huge margins. But I knew that the team had the talent to turn the table around. They just required some time and support to be competitive. I decided that I would be emphasizing on individual improvement areas and that too in the most painstaking way, which would then have an overall effect on the team's performance and not the other way around. I wanted to implement this approach carefully,' Dav says.

'It was really not a flash decision that all of us would go out and start winning games. More than any collective decision, it was a set of individual decisions, where every individual decided to raise his bar, where every individual realized that he could do better and started performing at a higher level. As individuals started performing better, it initiated a rub-off effect. Everyone started vying for higher targets. So, our winning team was all about a set of individuals who had maximized their potential,' comments Rahul Dravid.

Open Source leadership focuses on individuals. It not only gives them opportunities to maximize their potential unhindered, but also nurtures them to realize these—by embracing mentoring and coaching as serious day-to-day practices rather than as management fads. This is again rather different from the typical management approaches followed in traditional closed organizations—one that builds up hierarchies—where higher levels would supervise the levels under them, not as individuals with separate identities but as herds, to ensure productivity and results.

'It is up to the captain, the coach and the senior members to set the standards, to treat everyone differently. To identify each one's strengths,' Rahul adds. 'Juniors learn how to deal with others, and how to create a coaching culture from the environment that is set by the seniors. It starts from a few and spreads to the rest.

'A coach's job is to identify and build on the unique competencies of every player. This is not easy because part of a coach's job is to be able to communicate differently with different sorts of players with the single aim of enabling the team to win. What a coach provides to one player would be different from what he would for another. He must be able to provide the right thing at the right time at the right level.'

Step one to individual competency building: A coach's main and probably only job is to identify and build on the unique competencies of every player.

'In cricket, a coach's role also varies depending on the level he is coaching. At the lowest rung, he is telling you how to grip a bat, how to hold a ball, how to transfer your weight as you lean forward or how to position the seam. When the player, having learnt the basics, moves up the ladder, the coach's role changes drastically. Now he is watching the player bat or bowl for hours, meticulously making notes, trying to iron out the chinks in his armour, encouraging him to play shots when he is being overly subdued, asking him to pipe down when he is overly aggressive. He is reminding the player about the basics and, most importantly, training his mind—more a guide than a teacher. At the international level, however, technique usually needs only fine-tuning, so the coach's main job is to methodically analyse and interpret data obtained from actual match situations. He could draw a bowler's attention to the tendency to stray onto middle and leg over a sustained period; he could advise a batsman on specific tactics to upset the rhythm of a particular opposition bowler.

'But one thing is clear,' says Dav. 'It is the players who make a coach rather than the other way round because they are the ones who have to go to the battlefield. It is their battle. The coach creates an environment where the best in each player can come out. At the same time the coach can also go only up to a point where the player wants to. The player draws the line. So, it is the coach's responsibility to understand the individual temperaments and cater accordingly.'

A player makes a coach. A coach can go only up to the point where the player wants to.

Swami Pragyapath remembers that Sri Sri Ravi Shankar was able to reach out to him and make him feel special, even in the midst of a crowd thronging him on the very first day of their meeting. Every day henceforth, Sri Sri has made sure that he added value to Pragyapath's life in the most sensitive and intimate ways—evoking his conscience, helping him build on his strengths and improve on his weaknesses.

Pragyapath has been at the ashram for several years, but he says he still feels the same connect and intensity with his guruji as he felt on the first day. The ashram has grown multifold, the disciples have spread out to millions across the globe, but Sri Sri still reaches out to his individual and unique requirements, making him feel every day as if he was the most important person in the ashram.

Interestingly, Vikram Hazra voices the same opinion. He is another senior member in the ashram, who teaches many corporates and takes care of more than 500 villages. Yet, Sri Sri finds time to guide him, even if he traverses through the slightest distress. As an afterthought, Vikram adds that the time which guruji spends with him has actually reduced—because the ashram has grown to a level where several seniors vie for his time. Nevertheless, he never felt this because he has been mentored to extract the same quality of interaction in a reduced amount of time.

Vikram feels that this kind of growth is not possible if the mentor tries to keep the student under his wings all the time. The mentor should be able to take care of the needs of his people, but at the same time elevate them to the next level. Which Vikram suggests is a trade-off between the quality and quantity of time spent. As a mentorship relation starts, the mentor has to spend more time to have a certain quality of impact. But as the relationship grows, he would be able to develop a connect in such a way that the student would be able to exact more even in a shorter amount of time.

Step two to individual competency building: A coach should build a strong bond with his student. He should know the exact moment to step up.

Why the best coach is a father figure

Mentoring in Open Source leadership is not only about helping individuals develop their potential that is useful for their growth in the organization, but also about those aspects that might not have any implication on their professional life. According to Vikram Hazra, mentoring is never complete if it is restricted to one aspect of an individual's life. 'Is not our personal lives intertwined inseparably with our professional lives? Is it ever possible that we shut out all our personal problems the minute we step into our office? If that is the case, how can mentoring be restricted only to your professional realm? Guruji takes an interest even in our personal lives. In fact, he once asked me about three different people in a week—to help them find spouses. It is not that any one of these people approached guruji for help. But he, as their mentor, is interested in their overall growth. He realizes that when people lead happy lives, they would also be happy in their spiritual lives. So he guides us in acquiring the critical skills required for succeeding in what we do. At the same time, he also sits with us and takes a genuine interest in our personal issues.'

'Sourav never separated our personal lives from our actual performance on the field. He took an interest in our personal lives and he gave us some useful advice whenever we had troubles at home,' says Bhajji. 'At times I think he really understood me as a person and used that understanding to mould my performance. For example, I play better when I am in an angry mood. I take out my anger by focusing all my emotions on my bowling. This temperament has its own downsides in the field and in the dressing room. However, instead of taking that as a flaw, he sharpened my focus to use that to produce results and not to produce heartburn. He understood my personality and worked on it so that we could win. Whenever I was moody and my emotions were not focused, he would come up to me. He would empathize with my mood swings, and would direct it to the right context.'

Step one to parenting: Take a personal interest in the lives of your people.

'That is very important,' continues Bhajji. 'You could be an international player. But you have your own temperament. There are times you don't feel confident about yourself, especially when things are not going on as per your plan. But someone who is genuinely interested in mentoring you would be by your side then. It is more like a parent–child relationship than a sheer results-led professional one.'

Dav agrees to that. He says that a coach, more than anything else, has to be a caring parent to his people. 'It is good to convince yourself that you are being utterly professional and hence have to take a detached viewpoint of everything. But at the end of the day we need to realize that we are dealing with people in flesh and blood with real emotions. They respond to love and care. Once they know that you have a genuine interest in them, they start responding to your inputs.'

Dav is not talking in the air. He really has hard results to back up his theory. Compared to other famous and more established cricketers turned coaches like Greg Chappell and Javed Miandad, who adopted an absolutely professional approach towards the players, Dav stands out with the fabulous turnarounds that he has produced.

Vikram reiterates that the biggest reason for the enormous success of Art of Living is the fact that his guruji has always been taking a parental approach towards his people. 'It is never an employer–employee relationship. If it were, most of us would not have been here. He cares about me, and so I care about him.' So what does that mean? It means someone is interested in you beyond all short-term results. Someone is willing to be with you irrespective of whether things are going according to his expectations or not. However, a lot of us go wrong when we try to nurture people under us. As long as things are going according to a set plan, we are willing to risk things. But when they are not, we show our true colours—we either blame our people or we throw tantrums. But that sends out the exact opposite signals to your people. You need to be genuinely caring, irrespective of results.'

Step two to parenting: Genuinely care about your people, irrespective of results.

Dav confirms that this approach has helped him produce results. He says it is important that a coach proceeds slowly; that he does not take any abrupt actions or drive hasty changes. Dav follows a good rule to make sure that he is never misled into the path of hurried changes. And he calls this rule 'Being progress-minded rather than results-minded'. So what is this rule? 'Being focused on progress means not judging a person by the yardstick of wins or losses, rather defining milestones which he could grow to meet. Because coaching is not only about helping people with their techniques, on things like how to bat, but also giving the confidence that he could go out there and bat brilliantly. It is a slow, growth-oriented, confidence-building procedure. The student feels comfortable because his world is not changing abruptly, but at the same time he can see the progress that he is making.

'Once you make progress, in skills and in mental attitude, it is easier to go from there to real-time results. And once you emphasize individual improvement, it is easier to have an overall effect on the team's performance.'

Step three to parenting: Be progress-oriented than results-oriented.

In Open Source leadership, the role of a coach is not restricted to coaching, but it varies from a mentor to an instructor, assessor, advisor, supporter, counsellor, teacher—all the roles that a parent plays in your life—developing in you a trust as well as an attachment, which is one of the reasons why Open Source leadership organizations enjoy a lower level of employee turnover. Kiran Mazumdar Shaw has a case in point when she says that though most of her people stay along for life, some of them do fall prey to higher offers from her competitors, especially the younger ones. 'Salaries could be higher, but the atmosphere could never be reproduced. Hence, they start missing it. They start missing the people who nurtured them. We have many cases where they decided to come back.' But does she take them back? 'Of course, where is the question of not taking back a family member who has come back after straying around a bit?' she asks.

Step four to parenting: Be a true parent. Forgive and forget mistakes.

However, this attachment could also become a millstone around an organization's neck at times, where people get used to a certain style of coaching and refuse to adapt. A good example of this is that of John Wright, who was the coach of the Indian national cricket team from the year 2000 to 2005. John formed a wonderful mentoring partnership with Sourav as well as the other senior players in the team, where they took the juniors under their wings to eventually build up a world-beating team. Rahul Dravid says John played the role of a responsible parent, where he went beyond the call of duty to understand each player, giving them time and attention, at the same time working along with them in improving their performance. Eventually, John's tenure ended and the position was taken over by Greg Chappell—a strict results-driven disciplinarian. Though Greg brought with him some enormous experience and credibility as a world-renowned cricketer, compared to John, unfortunately they did not translate into results. He was not able to convince the team to go along. Soon there was discontentment and murmurings. The team performance fell to the lowest abyss when India crashed out of the World Cup—a championship where they were the finalists the previous time.

Techniques, skills, processes, all those mechanical things are important while coaching, but a good parental mentor and the chemistry that he builds up scores far higher results, especially in open organizations which are used to and which expect this kind of a style.

Why things that are going wrong, if left so, can produce miraculous results

Yet, things that are going wrong have an important role to play while people are being mentored in Open Source leadership. Dav says that true understanding between the coach and the player takes time to develop. 'It takes a bit of experience and encounters before one can be smart enough to learn and to be encouraged. It does not happen easily because there is a personal understanding required over here.'

Ironically, a crisis, especially early on in a relationship, can be a very good teacher for both sides. If a team starts winning right away after the coach takes charge, either because they were well prepared, or because circumstances were in their favour, it could make them miss out many subtler aspects. They could miss out on those details that could help them build up a long-term winning team. Exposure to pressurized situations, stressful conditions or even a massive loss, especially in the initial stages, can help a good coach to build a stronger and highly resilient team.

Mohammed Kaif, another important member in Sourav Ganguly's winning team, chips in with his own learning during the early stages of team formation. The team confidence at that point of time was almost at its lowest phase with match-fixing controversies looming large, and consecutive losses in series. It could not have been a more difficult situation. However, this low phase made it imperative that the senior members of the team as well as the supporting staff spent more time with the youngsters— analysing the situation as well as pushing up the game as a whole. The challenge was to turn around the losing streak, in whatever little ways.

Kaif says about his experience, 'This low phase made sure that we were closer to our senior members than ever before. We knew that we had nothing to lose but everything to gain. We had to make progress inch by inch—in batting, bowling and in fielding. At the same time, we also had to make sure that every individual in the team understood what was possible and what was not—by himself as well as by others in the team. So, one of the decisions that we made was not to be too bothered about winning and losing, at least in the short term, rather to go out there and do our individual best. That was good for the team, because we started understanding the potential as well as limits of each other. With the help of a coach and captain, we started to align accordingly. We experimented on our approaches—our batting and bowling line-ups, how we would handle specific situations like batting first or bowling first. Slowly, a great team started to build up. As we emerged out of this phase we had this strong self-belief that none of the other sides could beat us because we had been winning in the most difficult of situations.'

A low phase can be the best coach. It can bring the team together.

'A difficult situation can really help you improve together, if you are supported well by your coach, captain and senior players,' continues Kaif. If you look at the Indian team performance, you would notice that after about a year of going through a rough patch, we started peaking. An interesting observation in this is that not only the team, but also individuals peaked almost at the same time. If you look at my career graph, you could see that I had a patchy phase initially, with an occasional outstanding performance backed up by ordinary batting. In about a year, I was playing well. I scored well in the 2002 NatWest Series Final and won the Man of the Match award. Sehwag rose to prominence at almost the same time, in 2001. In the series victory over Australia in 2001, Harbhajan established himself as the team's leading spinner by taking thirty-two wickets and becoming the first Indian bowler to take a hat-trick in Test cricket. Zach again peaked during the same time. We went through fire together and we emerged out of it together.'

Zach agrees with this. He says the tough time they went through together helped them to be more open-minded to mentoring. Everyone was flexible and ready to be moulded. He even narrates an incident of how Sourav encouraged him to break the mould, even as he was assigned to bowl the slog overs. Typically, a bowler takes help and suggestions from other bowlers while dealing with tough situations. But Zach was asked to go up to the batsmen and discuss with them about what they go through and how they handle these overs. That experience helped Zach get under the skin of the batsmen, to better understand their psychology and how they behaved. 'That changed my perspectives about how people behaved in low situations,' says Zach.

A low phase can open up unconventional learning opportunities.

So, what are the things that mentors should keep in mind as they handle their students during stressful times? According to Dav, a coach should never sit back on lows nor should he start blaming individuals during times of losses. If he does so, that would have exactly the opposite effect, because the players would increasingly lose their confidence and the downslide would become more intense. For a good coach, a bad time is a time to avoid all emotions and snap decisions, to analyse the reasons for failure and how it could be overcome the next time around. 'A good coach does not go overboard, whether it is a loss or a win. He uses a loss to transform the team towards a win, and he uses a win to create more wins. A good coach makes sure that the culture of coaching is all-pervasive—across his people and across situations.'

Avoid all emotions and snap decisions after a loss.

Vikram Hazra sums it up in a philosophical manner. 'When I look at myself, at times I think that I have not changed, but when I look carefully into myself, from the day I came to this place till today, I find that I am a totally different person. My weaknesses are slowly being weeded out, while my strengths are reinforced multifold. Not just I, but everyone here is going through it every day, as you mentor and are being mentored. We are searching for solutions, we are learning to stand on our feet, we are confident that we are better people—every day. So profound that now it happens without any effort—like leaves fall without any effort in autumn. That is what this culture of coaching has done for us.'

Guaranteed Nail-biting Finish
Open Source Leadership Creates Constant Challenges to Keep Up the Momentum

In this section:
- Why in order to build an organization, you should try to destroy it
- How everyday challenges can push the envelope from all corners
- Three great tragedies and three steps to surmount them
- The bigger the challenge, the greater the impact: The art of building mass challenges
- Why challenges work in reiterating Open Source leadership
- Four steps towards constructing better organizational challenges

Why in order to build an organization, you should try to destroy it

The year was 1984. A young man named Shri sat at his desk and gazed out into the vast expanse of empty wilderness right outside his office trying to come up with a solution to the latest challenge that Kiran had swirled at him. He knew that if his company, Biocon, had to grow and achieve the heights that they were all dreaming about, they had to have a computer. But Kiran Mazumdar Shaw, his boss, was very clear. Being a start-up with many other financial priorities, a computer would be the last thing that they should be thinking about. 'If you desperately need a computer, it's your challenge to find the money for it,' she said unequivocally.

Tackling challenges, small and big, is a way of life with Open Source leadership. In fact, setting up and dealing with challenges is one methodology that these organizations use to promote openness in them. Everyday challenges that their seniors and peers hurl at them, along with a zillion others that they discover for themselves ensure that there is more social capital building up inside, people are sharing a vision, they are remaining aligned even in the absence of rules, and most importantly, they are going ahead and exploring their fullest potential.

Kiran believes that the true openness at the workplace starts with employees feeling a sense of ownership. 'I tell all my employees to own their jobs. When I say own your job, I mean owning all the problems that come along with it. In a normal company, owning a task is all about doing what the company's management is telling you to do, or doing what the boss expects you to do. But Biocon is very different. Here job ownership is all about solving problems because I always see that when people are tackling challenges, they are engaged better and are attached better—to the problem, to the team and to the company.'

Pragyapath has an incident from his own life to share. 'When I was a junior in the ashram, we had a project where we had to deal with some agencies in Delhi. We had an associate there, whom I was relying on to make sure that the work was being done. However, instead of easing the whole process, the project was getting delayed between the agencies and the associate. I knew that it could proceed much faster if I travelled to Delhi. Somehow, I felt that no one would allow me to, and hence I never asked anyone, nor did I take a decision myself.

'As the project was not completed, questions were asked. I naturally started blaming the agencies. But in no time fingers were pointed back at me, on why I did not visit Delhi. And why I did not take complete ownership of the project. "Has anyone stopped you?" asked guruji. In a way, he was making me realize that the system would never block me as long as my mind was not blocked. If I owned the task as my own, there was nothing that could stop me.'

Chanda Kochhar narrates an incident, a rather serious one, which could have even wrecked the bank, if it had not been taken care of at the right time. 'Once there was a huge run on our ATMs in Gujarat. Soon the news spread and anxious customers started crowding around our branches. We were on the job, monitoring the situation minute by minute including how much was getting withdrawn from each ATM and where the cash storage was lying so that we could move cash overnight to these ATMs. However, the bank managers were getting very jittery. The typical tendency is to pull the shutter down, nevertheless a bad one because that makes the customers more anxious. Instead, I requested the managers to go out there and talk to the customers. Initially, they were a bit apprehensive, because they feared the mob. But, as they went out there, to be with the customers rather than insulating themselves, the realization of ownership dawned upon them. It was no longer another task that they were asked to perform by their senior, but they owned the situation and hence it was their responsibility to take action. Some of the managers were even offering customers water to drink and making them comfortable. That sent the right message to the customers, who soon understood that it was unnecessary panic.'

Teach your people to take ownership of their tasks and of their roles.

'A perfectly defined task would never bring out the true potential in people. It takes far greater efforts than performing mindless tasks every day to create an excitement. True potential emerges only when people are exposed to challenges; challenges that they thought they could never solve. As they face these challenges in an organizational atmosphere they suddenly start thinking outside their everyday boxes.

'The moment you start viewing a problem as a challenge, you would give of your best to solve it. You are far more alert, far more resourceful and you apply your mind far more intelligently than you usually do. And the moment you solve it, you are confident. You say, "Wow, I never thought I could do that." Success over challenges drives every individual, and that is exactly what drives people in an open system—the drive to surmount challenges, the drive to achieve,' says Kiran.

How everyday challenges can push the envelope from all corners

In Open Source leadership, leaders realize that their people come from a variety of backgrounds, especially carrying along with them a bundle of previous experiences and thought processes, many a time limiting their true potential, and limiting their full involvement in the new model. Hence, a great challenge that these leaders face is to continually help their people to break out of these. Essentially, they do this by thinking up challenges which are relevant to each individual, to help them shed their limiting behaviours.

Charu works at the Art of Living Bureau of Communication. She has an interesting story to share in this context, which she believes changed her life forever. Charu came from a corporate background where she enjoyed a great lifestyle alongside other perks. But what was in store for her at the ashram surprised her. She was allocated a small dingy room which she had to share with five other people. Never used to such a situation, she found it unbearable. Her repeated requests for a single room were also turned down due to lack of availability. 'Though I went through one of the bleakest times in my life, eventually, things started looking up,' she says. The people with whom she shared space were helpful, and once she knew them better, she started feeling good. About a couple of weeks later, she had a chance to meet up with guruji, who to her surprise, enquired specifically about her stay and how she was adjusting. 'Only then did I understand that this was a challenge for me to get adjusted to the ashram way of life. I was allotted a single room afterwards, but by then I was comfortable with myself, the people around and the ashram. I was prepared.'

'In the ashram, our perceived weaknesses or limitations were never allowed to interfere with what we could truly achieve. We called this our grinding and polishing phase. For example, when I initially came over here, we did not have an introductory video film of guruji. Since I was a journalist, I was given that responsibility. I said fine! Three weeks planning, two months execution, budgeting, and then reviewing, we should be ready with our film in about six months. Then guruji gives me the shock of my life. He said that he would come back to see the finished film the day after. As I resisted, primarily because I knew how things work in the media world, he gave me five options that would really let me complete the film in the given time. That opened my boundaries. Interestingly, I completed the film in a couple of days, which is now called *Love Moves the World*. I still think it is one of the best I have ever made,' says Vikram Hazra.

Step one to pushing the envelope: Start from day one. Do not wait for the person to settle down for his first challenge.

But how did he do that? It is not easy to crunch six months of hard work into two days, that too to produce a work which is of high quality! Vikram has an answer to that. He says there are no fixed formulas or magic in there, but that we limit ourselves thinking 'this is the way it has to be done'. It is etched in our minds that we have to follow a certain route to get a certain quality output, while in reality there are a million other ways to do the same task. An open atmosphere just challenges you to open up an alternative path. It relieves you of any excuse that you could think of for shirking work, for delaying work or for playing below your potential.

'In my case, as I knew I had just two days to finish the film, I decided to rely on things that were already available as well as my skills. So, I went through old clips, identified what was useful, wrote the commentary, composed music and then hired a studio to complete it. And then sat down and wondered why anyone would take six months for something like this.'

In Open Source leadership, leaders focus on encouraging their people not to go down the risk-free and completely beaten track. They empower them to take continuous risks and embrace challenges. They invest in people by investing in new challenges for them. The logic behind this is simple. True potential emerges only when people are exposed to challenges; challenges that they thought they could never solve. As they face these challenges in an organizational context, they suddenly start thinking outside their everyday boxes. They are far more alert, far more resourceful and apply their minds far more intelligently than they usually do.

Step two to pushing the envelope: Discourage people from going down the beaten path. Open their minds to alternatives.

Most people today, especially in the professional world, play far below their potential, possibly because the tasks entrusted to them are of that nature, or because of the hidden glass ceilings. However, Open Source leadership surprises their people by letting them know what they could actually achieve. They use an interesting technique—'Technique of Insurmountable Challenges'—where the task is of such high magnitude that even the chances of failure are high.

Swami Pragyapath points out to a lovely white building called the Visalakshi Mantap, which is almost the focal point of the Art of Living ashram. This five-storeyed, lotus-shaped building with a thousand petals, blending Vedic architecture and modern technology is not only an architectural marvel but also a civil engineering feat. The glass dome that tops the building is adorned with a magnificent 'kalash' fifteen feet high—the biggest in Asia.

'Guruji wanted a meditation hall and asked me to handle the project. The interesting part of this story is that I do not have a civil engineering background at all. I am a chemical engineer by training,' says Pragyapath. 'In fact the whole world would have told him not to entrust me with this, because I was new in the ashram, and I was just twenty-six. I had no experience in construction, no experience in project management. I was totally raw. The project in itself had huge challenges. For example, the building had to be constructed without disturbing the ecology. We were not allowed to flatten the land, which was very uneven. The design had to represent all religions and their values. We had to engage local artists and artisans. And then there was the acoustics. In every way it had to be perfect.

'I spent four years on it. From a small meditation hall, the scope went up to a three-storeyed building and then to a five-storeyed. I made mistakes. However, he kept supporting me. We inaugurated the hall in January 2003. During the function, guruji asked me how much it cost us and I replied quoting the multimillions we had spent. However, he looked at me and said something that I least expected—that the whole money had not been spent on an inanimate infrastructure, but on my training,' remembers Pragyapath.

'That gave me a great insight—that for us human infrastructure is much more important than the physical ones. As I reflected on it, I recognized how much I had changed since that assignment. I was handling thirty-five contractors, close to 7,000 labourers, and craftsmen from all parts of the country, coordinating day-to-day activities and at the same time keeping an eye on the big picture.'

Step three to pushing the envelope: Use the advantage of the 'Technique of Insurmountable Challenges' to take your people to places where they have never been.

Three great tragedies and three steps to surmount them

All organizations exist in an environment where resources are limited in supply. Hence, it is imperative that for their longer sustenance and success they should behave in ways that can maximize the utilization of these. But individuals, quite different from the organizations as such, would not be worried. They would continue acting in ways that can further their self-interest rather than larger organizational interests, especially in case of smaller day-to-day decisions. If not checked, this tendency could be disastrous, where the interest of individuals directly clashed with that of the organization.

This organizational reality can be well explained through three theories. Though initially propounded for subjects as diverse as sociology, political science and psychology, these theories have strong reverberations in the field of management too.

The first one is the 'Tragedy of Commons', a theory derived from an influential article written by Geret Hardin, first published in the journal *Science* in 1968. The article describes a dilemma where multiple individuals acting independently in their own self-interest destroy a shared, limited resource, even when it is clear that it is not in anyone's long-term interest for this to happen. As a means of illustrating this, Hardin introduced a hypothetical example of a set of local herders sharing a common parcel of land (the commons), on which they were all entitled to let their cows graze. According to Hardin, it was in each herder's interest to put as many cows as possible onto the land, even if the commons would be irreversibly damaged as a result.' The utility of each additional animal had both a positive and a negative component. On the positive side, the herder received all the benefits from the additional cows. On the negative side, the pasture was slightly degraded by each additional animal. Therefore, while the individual herder gained all of the advantage, the entire group shared the disadvantage, which was the damage to the pasture. This clash between individual and larger interests leads to a tragedy—the tragedy of commons.

The second is the 'Theory of Public Choice', an economic theory primarily used to study problems that are traditionally in the province of political science.

The Public Choice theory is often used to explain how political decision making results in outcomes that conflict with the preferences of the public, because politicians and government officials are ultimately self-interested agents who are operating in a social system. For example, many special interest and pork barrel projects are not in the interests of the overall system. However, it makes perfect sense for politicians to support these projects. It can make them feel powerful and important. It can improve their image, increasing votes or campaign contributions. It can also benefit them financially—through kickbacks or by opening the door to future wealth as lobbyists. However, the politician pays little or no cost to gain these benefits, as he is spending public money. He has a rational incentive to do exactly what he is doing, even though the desire of the general constituency is the opposite.

The third one is 'Social Trap', a term first introduced by John Platt in the area of psychology. Building upon the concept of the 'Tragedy of Commons', Platt recognized that short-term avoidance behaviour by individuals could lead to a long-term loss for the entire group. Platt provided an anecdote (taken from an article written by Schelling in 1971) to elaborate his theory, where a mattress slipped unnoticed from the top of a car on to a two-lane highway. The easiest thing for any driver behind was to stop and pull the mattress to the side of the road. However, drivers seldom do that. Instead, they back up and go around the mattress, even if that means creating a traffic jam. Each individual driver avoids stopping and setting out of his car to pull the mattress to the side of the road—a small sacrifice for the greater good. The long-term consequence of this avoidance behaviour is that all of the drivers arrive at their destinations later than they would have if only one individual had removed the mattress barrier.

All these theories point out to one thing—that we humans are ultimately rational beings whose decisions are self-motivated, considering only those benefits and costs that directly affect us. This important point is equally applicable in organizational management as much as in other subjects. For example, corporate resources, like information technology, provided for through a centralized budget, are resources where the 'Tragedy of Commons' is in full-fledged action. Centralized operations separate users, be it individuals or business units, from costs, making it appear like a free resource for them. Since it is perceived as free, without any budget or resources going from them, they tend to overestimate their demands and then waste or underutilize these. On the other hand, as far as the department of information technology is concerned, they do not directly get the benefits, and hence do not have a direct incentive to be on top of their game. The result is a general dissatisfaction as well as wastage of common resources from both the parties.

Another example where the dynamics of 'Public Choice' theory is at work is among managers when it comes to assessment of their subordinates' performance and pay hikes. Most managers try pushing in the highest possible increases for their subordinates, even if that means overrating underperformances. Such activities help individual managers to justify their own performances, be one up over the other teams, and at the same time, increase their power and influence inside their teams. We also notice that managers constantly keep projecting and acquiring extra hands and resources, more than they would ever need, not only in anticipation of extra business but also because more subordinates can mean more power. The managers in these cases act exactly like the politicians in the 'Theory of Public Choice', where they unnecessarily waste valuable resources because they do not pay for them. Actions such as these serve the short-term interests of individuals but are detrimental to the performance of the company as a whole.

Social traps, again, operate around us all the time, as team members shy away from things that they can do to improve the performance, but would not do because no one told them to. They would limit their involvement strictly to whatever has been defined and to nothing else that would take either their time or their efforts. There are other typical examples of social traps, like a procurement manager who does not negotiate to the fullest because a better deal does not give him any specific advantage, though it is better for the organization.

'Exposing individuals to various challenges can make sure they are not wasting valuable resources—be it money, time or efforts,' claims Vijaya Menon. She has good data points to back up her claim, drawn from her experiences at Air Deccan. She comments that typical press conferences of companies cost them upwards of a million rupees, simply because there is less accountability and more wastage of common resources. Surprisingly, in the case of Air Deccan, it used to be in a few thousands. 'In our case, we did not have any budgets, but at the same time we could not avoid press conferences because those were a serious part of our marketing plan. How did we do this? By making sure that everyone was equally involved, irrespective of the department or location. We made sure that everyone owned the challenge with equal passion. We never had a PR agency, ever. We even minimized our travel to the location, but took turns to call up the press, the politicians and everyone else who needed to be contacted. We would do our conferences in our airport lounges. There would be a huge board, handouts, some coffee and some snacks. No five-star hotels or five-course dinners. Yet our press conferences used to generate more interest and results than any of those bigger events, simply because for each one of us, it was a challenge. It was an opportunity to prove that it could be done this way too.'

> Step one to tackling the tragedy: Minimize access to resources that could be wasted.

'Everyone in the organization was aligned to costs. We all knew that our individual existence depended on this. Whatever we did began with the cost question. Before any discussion, people asked. 'What are the costs?' That kept things in perspective,' adds Vijaya.

Step two to tackling the tragedy: Align the existence of individuals to the maximum utilization of limited resources.

Umesh, one of the senior members of Art of Living and the driver of Sri Sri, reminds us that resource crunch has never been a new situation at his ashram. He says that it has always been like this, in the past, when it was a handful of members, and now when it is millions of members. 'As we started out, the biggest problem that we faced was a shortage of rooms. There were more visitors coming in and not enough rooms. So everyone in the ashram was involved in finding solutions, in making sure that all were accommodated comfortably. Today we have close to 3,000 rooms. Yet, we are in the same position because the members have also grown multifold. Everyone is still involved in making sure that people are comfortable. It is an everyday, every-minute challenge that keeps everyone of us on our toes. We have to stretch every resource.'

The game of cricket has an interesting way in which they implemented challenges to stretch limited resources. Kaif says, 'I have always played well when I played higher in the line-up as the number three batsman because that position gave me time to settle down. However, usually I had to bat at number seven, since there were other specialist batsmen for the third position. Lower-down positions had their own challenges. Sourav understood this. I was told that if I faced thirty balls and scored thirty-five to forty runs, it would be as good as scoring a century. I had to utilize those few overs that I got to produce the maximum result for my team. My challenge was not to settle down in the pitch, but to score on every ball.'

Step three to tackling the tragedy: Give people a personal reason to better utilize organizational resources.

Kiran adds on with a different experience on how well positioned challenges can help in the maximum utilization of resources. 'Our real transformation came in 1979 as we acquired this site. We were looking around for properties to buy and suddenly this came up as a distress sale. But it came with a big challenge. It was almost in the wilderness, far away from any civilization. Every day it was a sheer challenge just travelling and reaching this place. It was also a great opportunity because all of us believed in the same thing. We would grow fast so that we could fill up our new-found place with our offices. We would build this place with our bare hands—brick by brick.'

Everyday challenges help Open Source leadership organizations handle the subtle yet tricky phenomenon of the 'Tragedy of Commons', 'Public Choice' and 'Social Traps'. By keeping access to resources at minimal levels, celebrating frugality as a virtue, linking individual sustenance to organizational growth, building individual accountabilities for every resource and by creating peer pressure on allocation and spending of every small resource, Open Source leadership makes sure that the utilization is always optimal.

The bigger the challenge, the greater the impact: The art of building mass challenges

Challenges also help in building social capital and in reducing the silos between departments. Organizational walls get broken down, as people who are given challenges reach out to others for help. However, there is another kind of challenge which Open Source leadership resorts to—'Mass Challenges'—a phenomenon quite different from individual challenges. Neither are they posed to individuals in the organization nor do they take into consideration the individual strengths and weaknesses. Instead, they are executed at a mass level. Although 'mass challenges' do help in serving the same purposes as individual challenges—creating ownership, raising aspirations and combating the 'Tragedy of Commons'—it contributes at a much higher level, in fact in some cases raising organizational bonding and aspirations multifold. This gives an opportunity for individuals to start fitting into an overall system, and to discover their strengths as a group.

Biocon has a case in point where they ended up facing a mass challenge—something which they had not taken into account. A great challenge arose in Biocon when the labourers, under the influence of some outsiders, decided to form a union in 1984. Kiran was taken by surprise, because as a company they always believed in giving the best as well as equal treatment to all their people. Although momentarily startled by their announcement, Kiran calmly attempted to reason with them. She was willing to help them, even by going out of her way. They accepted that they were fine with the company policies and happy with the ambience. However, they still wanted to form a union. As things started getting worse, workers squatted on the floors, brandished pickets, burnt effigies and started giving threatening calls to the leadership team.

'The challenge was of such proportion that none of the individuals or departments was able to handle it independently. So, we reached out to people across the organization. We would be in this together. Tasks that we had never done earlier, or we thought we would ever do, we did those together. The engineers, PhDs and managers from all departments and functions, all of us got down to doing unskilled jobs. For three months we did that, in the mean time working on alternatives. We remained focused as the union workers continued giving us a tough time. After many weeks we reopened a new sparkling automated Biocon,' says Murli Krishnan, group president, Finance.

At the same time, the incident also taught Kiran a new practical lesson. 'I realized that a system like ours would only work well if people were on the same wavelength, or if they were open about their differences and willing to reconcile. I was very naïve in hiring these unskilled people and expecting them to respond and be responsible for the challenges in the same way as the educated lot. There is a certain disconnect when you have someone uneducated, who is poor, whose trust in the rest of the society is less because he is deprived of resources.

'There is also a disconnect in terms of understanding the challenge itself. Suppose I tell my sweeping lady that I want this toilet to be very clean, she will do it literally because I am telling her to do it. She will not do it because that is the way she thinks it should be done. It would be very difficult for her to see the bigger challenge. For challenges that can build an open atmosphere, it is important that people trust each other and reach out to each other,' she says.

Step one to mass challenges: Social capital is the foundation upon which mass challenges are established.

Art of Living has another excellent incident to narrate the 'mass challenge' phenomenon, an incident that has been referred to as 'the moment' that changed the course of the organization—the silver jubilee celebrations. Held in February 2006, this mega event brought together almost 2.5 million people from over 145 countries including several heads of state, policy makers and industry leaders. A special dais spread over 3.5 acres was erected to stage the event. About 3,800 musicians took the centre stage to conduct a symphony with a range of Eastern and Western instruments. Security personnel, comprising about 2,000 policemen and 1,000 private security guards, were deployed to maintain order at the venue. A helipad was readied at the aerodrome for the landing of a dozen VIPs and dignitaries.

'The entire organization came together from the planning to the execution stage. We were all immersed in it for several months. Even then, nothing prepared us for the reality. When we saw it unravelling, we were simply awestruck. Until that time we were working, day and night, but never thought we would be able to pull off something as magnificent. However, what happened after this event was bigger than what happened during the event,' says Vikram.

'That event opened up the possibility for every individual within the organization. Most of us were stuck in the reality of day-to-day things. It just broke. And as it broke, individual potential exploded, and so did the organization. Till that time I was struggling to get fiifty people for my sessions in Bombay. After that event, I was teaching 5,000 people a session. My largest concert was 5,000 people and I was suddenly singing in front of a crowd of 50,000. We were celebrities overnight. A single incident opened up our potential. We were no longer thinking small. We were thinking about larger issues—someone started thinking of how to make Mumbai a cleaner place, somebody else on how to bring peace to the terrorism-hit areas, while someone else was thinking about organizing a Guinness record-making dance festival. It was a challenge that gave us results, which we could not have achieved in twenty years otherwise,' Vikram exclaims.

Step two to mass challenges: Use mass challenges to bring about huge organization-level transformations and not for solving smaller problems.

Why challenges work in reiterating Open Source leadership

Why do open leaders vouch by the efficacy of posing great challenges to their people? One of the reasons is that they have had their own experiences of the role challenges can play in planting and nurturing leadership experiences in a person. In my earlier book, *Decide to Lead*, I examined how certain challenging moments can become the 'defining moments' for a person—moments where a person comes to grip with the reality or weaves together several earlier instances in a way that makes real renewed sense. The crux of a defining moment is a decision to take charge of the situation and to lead. These defining moments are important, because they have the power to change the life of a person in such a way that it transforms the person and brings forth his hidden potential.

Some of the Open Source leadership founders are shining examples of how well-crafted challenges become their defining moments. Kiran is such a person. She considers herself an accidental entrepreneur because she never wanted to be one or thought she could be one. When she came back from Australia, qualified as a master brewer, her whole focus was on getting a job in a brewery. But then she met her first challenge. Though potential employers accepted that she was technically competent, they were extremely wary of giving a woman charge of a brewery. Instead, they were willing to give her smaller responsibilities.

Kiran was not satisfied. She thought they were underestimating her capabilities. It was at that point in time that she ran into Leslie Auchincloss, the founder of Biocon Biochemicals, Ireland, who had come to India looking for a partner for his venture. He was quick to identify the fire in her belly and offered her the partnership. Nevertheless, Kiran was more practical. It sounded exciting, yet she knew that she would not fit the role since she did not have a business background nor any capital. Moreover, she was also disillusioned by the fact that she could not yet find a job in India. 'If I cannot even get a job, how would I ever run a company,' she wondered. She was convinced that she would be a liability if she ever embarked on such a journey. However, Leslie would not be dissuaded. Instead, he gave her a challenge—to see this as an opportunity for her to show the world that she could be very successful, despite all the job rejections. With that challenge, Kiran faced her defining moment. She decided to start out on her journey as an entrepreneur and as a leader.

Challenges could motivate leadership choices in people by helping them face their defining moments.

Along her journey, Kiran decided to take a leaf out of Leslie's book—the art of posing challenges. She believes that good challenges have the potential to be defining moments for people—where people who were till then thought to be average turn around to reveal their true potential. 'I never thought I could ever do even a small percentage of what we are doing now. What happens if many more like me awaken to their potential?' Kiran asks in a matter-of-fact voice.

Like in Kiran's case, many Open Source leadership organizations are born as a result of great challenges. And in turn, they go ahead and set up greater challenges for themselves, to be surmounted to get to their vision. They weave larger visions that can make a real difference to the world. 'When the organizational objective itself is so large a challenge, how can individual tasks be of lesser proportion?' exclaims Vikram.

'What we wanted to achieve could be achieved only if each one of us rose beyond all expectations,' says Captain Gopinath, the founder of Air Deccan. 'We are a country of a billion people. We were poor because of this population. Our nation tackled it through fair price shops, subsidies, etc. We were hungry souls. One day as I was flying in a helicopter from Mangalore to Bangalore, I saw something reflecting from the rooftops. That piqued my curiosity. What was reflecting? They were large dish antennas on almost every rooftop. Suddenly, I sensed a note of diffidence and self-confidence in India. Instead of a billion hungry souls, I saw a billion hungry consumers.'Signs of consumerism were growing across the nation. Even as I went to villages, I could see these signs of consumerism—televisions, refrigerators. As I mulled over it, I realized that there was a demand for all sorts of things, but not airlines. Airline travel was still outside an Indian consumer's dream. They were not able to relate to it—just like most of us are not able to relate to someone who travels in a Rolls Royce. To add . to this, the then existing airlines, Jet Air and Indian Airlines, were for people who were travelling between metros. I said to myself that the future was not here, the future was in the other India. It was so obvious.

'We started out with one flight. And in three-and-a-half years we grew to 350 flights, one city to sixty-six cities. What Indian Airlines did in fifty-four years we did in three-and-a-half. We never competed with the other airlines, but with the railways. The thought process was simple. If Norway, which has a population about the same as Kanpur, can have twenty-five million passengers, if Singapore's airport can handle 113 flights, how much does India need for this kind of population? That was the first challenge. Every month we added an aircraft and four to five routes and we kept growing. We started the airlines with no money in our pockets, but from there, we raised a total of 250 million dollars. We had to fight a new challenge every day.

'Chief ministers and journalists identified with us because we stood for the common people. They saw us as their messiah. With one stroke, one day we created a social change. We broke the caste system. Earlier an officer would go by plane and a mechanic by train. The rich would travel by air and the middle class by rail. We changed that. Now the mechanic would travel alongside the officer, the barber alongside the businessman.'

> In Open Source leadership, a leader's vision itself is the biggest challenge that he should surmount.

Four steps towards constructing better organizational challenges

Adds Captain Gopinath, 'But to create that kind of trigger and explosion in the market, we had to be constantly on the hunt for challenges. The original plan was to have about six to eight aircraft at the end of two years. In the end, we had more than thirty aircraft. We grew up to the next challenge. We ordered for another ninety. We never went by the state of readiness. Even when things were not ready, we would just go ahead and announce it to the press. That put pressure on us, to make sure that we were meeting that deadline. We would announce routes before they were ready. Then we would run faster than ever before to get there. We strived to outperform, every day, every minute.'

Considering that these challenges are larger than life, what happens if individuals are not able to live up to the challenges? Are leaders supposed to guide them through every step? 'Not really,' says Vikram Hazra. 'Handling challenges is different from mentoring. Mentoring is hands on. A leader is supposed to be with his people, identifying and nurturing the unique competency of every player, being with them throughout the process like a caring parent. However, posing challenges is all about a hands-off process. A leader behaves almost like an autocrat, where he expects the individual to conquer his own challenges.'

Step one to setting challenges: Challenges demand the leader to be hands-off, compared to mentoring which is hands-on.

Chanda Kochhar agrees with this. 'When you move the bar higher, there is a chance that it would stretch people. But there is also a chance that they could break. A leader will have to keep watching to be sure that his or her challenges are making people taller and not breaking them. At the same time, the leader will also need to remain cautious to resist any temptation to take over the authority when things are going wrong. These are huge challenges, and hence leaders have to be patient enough to allow their people to learn from their mistakes. They should just extend their support during the rough spots instead of taking over. Taking over would kill a challenge forever.'

Step two to setting challenges: Resist your temptation to take over, even when things are going wrong.

'Challenges should be left to the individuals to surmount. A leader's role is to give everybody a full chance. That is the only way you can make sure that challenges are part of the individual as well as organizational DNA.' Vikram adds, 'Now that I have been in this system for so long, I no longer look at them as challenges. I just look at them as part of our physical and mental growth. There was a time when I felt a small crowd coming in for a course could be a challenge. Now, I am accustomed to it. Even if 20,000 people come in, I know we can rise up to that challenge. The caterpillar has to go through a tough time as a pupa before it can emerge as a butterfly.'

'People who want to achieve are always looking out for an environment that would help them do so. More than money, more than any designations, they aspire for challenges that they can surmount. Biocon realized that early, and we made sure that became part of our culture,' says Kiran.

Step three to setting challenges: Institutionalize challenges. Make them a part of your organizational DNA.

Biocon is no longer a small company. It is large and hugely successful—about 4,000 employees spread out in multiple locations, with a turnover of thousands of millions. It is the flag-bearer of biotechnology in India. However, no one rests at Biocon. They realize the task that perpetuating the same old DNA is tougher than it ever used to be, because of the sheer size and complexity of the organization.

'It is no longer easy to freely empower every single employee as it was when we were smaller. But at the same time, that in itself is a challenge—to continue to focus strongly on not going down the completely beaten track,' says Arun Chandavarkar.

As far as Kiran is concerned, she is made continually aware of the fact that there would be no dearth of challenges. 'The company is listed and every movement in the stock market is dissected and analysed. The challenges are bigger and more real now. It is not just people, but also profits.' At the same time she is also looking at issues that have far greater implications. She is currently looking at health care including health insurance and sanitation that can help our nation combat some of the greatest challenges that it is facing today.

> Step four to setting challenges: Finding bigger challenges than the earlier ones is tough. Nevertheless, open leaders still have to find them.

As far as Shri was concerned, who went on to become the president, R&D, of Biocon, he handled his challenge effectively by taking a Rs 30,000 loan from his grandfather to procure a computer for the company. Biocon eventually acquired that computer and repaid his loan.

Conclusion
When Will Others Follow Suit?

10

In this section:
- Why Open Source leadership is not only populist but also practical
- When will others follow suit?

Why Open Source leadership is not only populist but also practical

Any new idea that favours the underdogs compared to the top dogs tends to gain popularity in the short term. However, the real success of these ideas depends not on their populism, but how they perform and deliver value vis-à-vis the existing ideas. Ideas, like democratic nation states and egalitarian families, stand exactly because of this—that they are able to bring in more value to the social contexts that they operate in. Open Source leadership is such an idea. It is the inevitable future of organizations and leadership, again not because it is populist, but because it is able to bring in substantially more value compared to the existing traditional closed formats of leadership. In the new age—where organizations and leadership face enormously complicated environments and high expectations from all quarters—Open Source leadership enables them to be more successful by opening up power and authority associated with leadership to all the levels of the organization.

However, Open Source leadership can prima facie appear to be utopian because of our continued hobnobbing with the traditional closed systems. Yet, as days go by, we are increasingly discovering that this conventional system is not without flaws.

We are increasingly realizing that what it took to manage then is not what it takes to manage now. This is why it is important to recognize these few organizations and leaders who have emerged as forerunners in the practice of Open Source leadership.

These organizations, as we saw in the earlier chapters, are resetting the definitions of power to fit in all the people who are involved, and not just the traditional 'leader'. They are not only eliminating the traditional roles associated with leadership, but are also actively providing incentives to their people to embrace more power and authority—be it by way of reiterating constant trust in them, or by way of ensuring complete transparency, or by creating an environment where constant excitement is a way of life.

They are also doing this by redefining some of our conventional thoughts—like complementing the formal management mechanisms with informal coordination mechanisms like coffee table conversations, or by breaking down the traditional workplace maps, or even by aligning the personal goals of people alongside the organizational vision.

When will others follow suit?

However, the bigger question here is, now that a few have taken the lead, when will the majority of our organizations shift towards Open Source leadership? John Maxwell has a rather philosophical take on this. 'There are three instances that can prompt more of today's traditional organizational leaders to embrace Open Source leadership. The first is when they have suffered enough so that now they have no option but to open up. For example, the high-handedness and short-sightedness of some of the so-called leaders are resulting in catastrophes like financial irregularities and bankruptcies, affecting not just the organization but also the whole economy. The more that leaders go through such situations, the more they would be willing to open up. A second instance is when leaders learn enough about the concept so that they want to change. For example, when traditional closed leaders meet up with leaders from Open Source leadership organizations, they learn about the enormous success they have had with the concept. They suddenly realize that there are possibilities beyond traditional closed management techniques. Such learning has a huge impact on leaders, especially when coming from their peers who are more successful. The third instance is when leaders have received enough so that they are able to open up. As more people come to leaders and as more resources are made available to them, they become more aware of the fact that they do not have the ability to manage everything themselves, that they need the help of others around them. They realize that the only way to grow further is by making sure that they open up to more people.

'In the new business era—with its own set of contradictions— where on one side we have an environment which is getting complicated by the day, and on the other, with technology increasingly opening up every bit of information, we would all be practising Open Source leadership sooner than expected,' says Maxwell.

Tony Hsieh's thoughts are on similar lines. He says, 'Today's marketplace is very different from yesterday's. Earlier, only the large players would have been able to sustain themselves in the market. So, being large was an advantage. But today, it is not so. Nimbleness and agility are the coveted qualities. A start-up operating from a garage could threaten you as much as a multi-billion-dollar empire.' This new scenario instigates change because leaders realize that traditional management methods will not help them withstand competition. They realize that only by letting people truly play at their highest potential can companies create maximum value. This will force more corporations and CEOs to ease up and open up.'

Noam Chomsky sums it up well: 'We are headed right there. It is just a matter of time.'

References

Accountable-workplace.com, 'Why the Manager's Role Must Change', accessed on 15 June 2009.

Acemoglu, Daron, and James Robinson, *Economic Origins of Dictatorship and Democracy*, New York: Cambridge University Press, 2006.

Advancinginsights.com

Ajula.edu

Alderman, Naomi, 'Encarta's Failure is No Tragedy', *The Guardian*, 7 April 2009.

Alesina, Alberto, and Eliana La Ferrara, 'Participation in Heterogeneous Communities', *The Quarterly Journal of Economics*, MIT Press, Vol. 115 (3), pp. 847–904, August 2000.

_____. 'Who Trusts Others?', *Journal of Public Economics*, Elsevier, Vol. 85(2), pp. 207–34, August 2002.

Allacademic.com

Allbusiness.com

Allis, Ryan, *Zero to One Million*, New York: Virante, 2003.

Altfeldinc.com

Amble, Brian, 'Not So Much a Glass Ceiling as a Glass Cliff', http://www.management-issues.com, accessed on 6 September 2004.

Anderson, Dave, 'Three Keys to Accountability', *Agency Sales*, 1 October 2003.

Andrewartha, Jeanee, 'Ricardo Semler—Seven Day Weekend', retrieved from passioncomputing.com.au, on 3 September 2009.

Anfuso, Dawn, 'Turning Business into a Game', *Personnel Journal*, pp. 50, 1 March 1995.

_____. 'Springfield Remanufacturing Corp', https://www.workforce.com, accessed on 3 September 2009.

Annamária, Toth, 'Workplace Mentoring System', https://www.Artima.com, accessed on 3 September 2009.

Acker Ashley, 'Ricardo Semler: Management Renegade', workstyledesign/blog, accessed on 11 March 2009.

Avritzer, Leonardo, 'Public Deliberation at the Local Level: Participatory Budgeting in Brazil', *Universidade Federal de Minas Gerais*, Fall 1999.

Baiocchi, Gianpaolo, 'Participation, Activism, and Politics: The Porto Alegre experiment and Deliberative Democratic Theory', paper delivered at the Experiments for Deliberative Democracy Conference, November 1999.

Bandiera, Oriana, Iwan Barankay, and Imran Rasul, 'Cooperation in Collective Action', *Economics of Transition*, Vol. 13, No. 3, pp. 473–98, July 2005.

Banffcentre.ca

Bardsley, Nicholas, *Dictator Game Giving: Altruism or Artefact*, Hampshire: National Centre for Research Methods, University of Southampton, 2008.

Bares, Ann, 'The Tragedy of the Commons and Merit Pay', Compforce. typead.com, accessed on 21 May 2008.

Battilana, Silvia Console, 'Why Did the Mafia Emerge in Italy? An Institutional Answer', Research paper written in November 2003.

Ber, Adrian, 'Motivation in Open Source', http://beradrian.wordpress. com/2008/11/27/motivation-in-open-source/, accessed on 27 November 2008.

Beradrian.wordpress.com

Bitzer, Jurgen, and J.H. Philipp, *The Economics of Open Source Software Development*, Elsevier Science, 2006.

Bolt, Jim, *The Learning Glass Ceiling (or, is your leader a Know it All?)*, New York: The Fast Company, 7 February 2008.

Brenner, Reuven, *The Financial Century: From Turmoils to Triumphs*, Toronto: Stoddart, 2001.

Broadstuff.com

Bromley, Peter, *The Best of the Best Report*, Toronto: First Light PMV Inc., 2003.

Brookes, Donald, 'Who's Accountable for Accountability?', *Canadian Manager*, 22 June 1992.

Brown, Bob, 'Governance of Information Technology: Avoiding the Tragedy of the Commons', *Journal of Health Care Management*, Vol. 16, No. 4, 30 December 2001, pp. 10–11.

Buckmaster, Sharon, 'Shared Leadership: What is it, Why is it Important, and Who Wants it Anyway?' KA9 Overview Paper, 3 January 2004.

Businessweek.com

Cape.org

Caulkin, Simon, 'Who's in Charge Here? No One', *The Observer*, 27 April 2003.

Chafkin, Max, 'The Zappos Way of Managing', https://www.Inc.com, accessed on 21 May 2009.

Chanrith, Ngin, 'Strengthening NGO Accountability through Beneficiary Participation: Lessons Learned from Two Cambodian NGOs', published by Graduate School of International Development. Nagoya University, February 2004.

Civil Society Accountability: 'Who Guards the Guardians?', lunchtime address delivered by Kumi Naidoo, at the UN Headquarters in New York, 3 April 2003.

CNN.com, 'An Interview with AirAsia's CEO', http://edition.cnn.com/2004/TRAVEL/07/16/bt.airasia.ceo.intv/index.html, accessed on 26 July 2004.

CNN.com, 'Interview with Tony Fernandes', http://www.cnn.com/2007/WORLD/asiapcf/09/20/talkasia.fernandes/index.html?iref=newssearch, accessed on 24 October 2007.

Coachingclasses.co.in

Connolly, John, 'Real Transparency will Break the Glass Ceiling', *Personnel Today*, 28 September 2004, p. 29.

Conradt, L., and T.J. Roper, 'Group Decision-Making in Animals', *Nature*, Vol. 421, 9 January 2003, pp. 155–58.

Conradt, L., J. Krause, 'Leading According to Need in Self-Organizing Groups', www.princeton.edu/~couzin/Conradtetal2009.pdf, accessed on 3 March 2009.

Conradt, Larissa, and Christian List, 'Group Decisions in Humans and Animals: A Survey', *Philosophical transactions of the Royal Society of London*, Series B, Biological sciences, Vol. 364, No. 1518, pp. 719–42, 2009.

Corstange, Dan, 'Culture and Organizational Structure: An Agent-Based Model', paper presented at the annual meeting of the Midwest

Political Science Association, Palmer House Hilton, Chicago, Illinois, 15 April 2004.

Das, Gurcharan, 'Why the Future Belongs to India', *The Times of India*, 10 May 2009.

Deiss, Kathryn J., and George Soete, 'Developing Shared Leadership: A Note for a New Year', *ARL Newsletter*, December 1997.

Deutschman, Alan, *The Un-CEO*, http://www.fastcompany.com/magazine/98/wikn.html, accessed on 19 December 2007.

Doyle, Michele, and Mark Smith, 'Shared Leadership', http://www.infed.org/leadership/shared_leadership.htm, accessed on 19 February 2009.

Drath, W., *The Deep Blue Sea: Rethinking the Source of Leadership*, San Francisco: Jossey-Bass, 2001.

Dudwick, Nora, Kathleen Kuehnast, 'Analyzing Social Capital in Context: A Guide to Using Qualitative Methods and Data', World Bank Institute, 2006.

Dunn, Wayne, 'Majority Rule: The Tyrants Next Door', http://capitalismmagazine.com, accessed on 25 September 2009.

Eberlei, Walter, 'Accountability in Poverty Reduction Strategies: The Role of Empowerment and Participation', World Bank, *Social Development Papers*, Paper No. 104, May 2007.

Economist, 'Animal Behaviour: Decisions, Decisions', 13 February 2009.

Economist, 'Out of Anarchy', 17 February 2000.

Edu.blogs.com

Elliott, Timo, 'Fixing the BI Tragedy of the Commons', timoelliott.com/blog, accessed on 17 September 2007.

Esteban, Monza, and Debraj Ray, 'On the Measurement of Polarization', *Econometrica*, Econometric Society, Vol. 62(4), July 1994, pp. 819–51.

Evans, Philip, and Bob Wolf, 'Collaboration Rules', *Harvard Business Review*, July 2001, pp. 96–104.

F3strategies.org

Factoryjoe.com, 'The Future of Open Leadership', http://factoryjoe.com/blog/2006/06/15/the-future-of-open-leadership/, accessed on 18 September 2009.

Farrell, Henry, and Jack Knight, 'Trust, Institutions, and Institutional Change: Industrial Districts and the Social Capital Hypothesis', *Politics and Society*, Vol. 31 No. 4, December 2003, pp. 537–66.

Farrell, Henry, 'Social Capital in Action!' http://crookedtimber. org/2007/09/25/social-capital-in-action/, accessed on 25 September 2007.

Feller, Joseph, Brian Fitzgerald, *Perspectives on Free and Open Source Software*, Cambridge, Massachusetts: MIT Press, 2005.

Fienberg, Howard, 'A Review of Making Democracy Work, a Book by Robert Putnam', http://www.hfienberg.com/irtheory/putnam.html, accessed on 6 June 2009.

Fischer, Gerhard, 'Social Creativity: Making All Voices Heard', retrieved from Colorado.edu, 2005.

Fischer, Gerhard, Eric Scharff, and Ye Yunwen, 'Fostering Social Creativity by Increasing Social Capital', http://l3d.cs.colorado.edu/~gerhard/ papers/social-capital-2002.pdf, accessed on 11 September 2009.

Fisher, Anne, 'Piercing the "Bamboo Ceiling"', retrieved from money. cnn.com, posted on 8 August 2005.

Fisher, Lawrence, 'Ricardo Semler Won't Take Control', posted on strategy-business.com on May 2008.

Fishman, Charles, 'Engines of Democracy', retrieved from http://www. fastcompany.com/magazine/28/ge.html?page=0%2C0, Posted on 19 December 2007.

Flora, Cornelia, 'Building Social Capital: The Importance of Entrepreneurial Social Infrastructure', dgroups.org/file2.axd/9cccfd87.../Building_ Social_Capital.doc, accessed on 18 June 2009.

Footdown.com

Forbes.com

Fourmilab.ch

Freesoftwaremagazine.com

Fukuyama, Francis, 'Social Capital and Civil Society', The Institute of Public Policy, George Mason University, 1 October 1999.

Fuller, Rebecca, 'Explaining "Why" Builds Accountability', http:// findarticles.com/p/articles/mi_m3495/is_5_50/ai_n13721376, accessed on 1 May 2008.

Fundinguniverse.com

Gallagher, Robert A., 'Shared Leadership: The Maintaining of Task and Relationship Functions', http://www.orgdet.com/shared_leadership. htm, accessed on 11 September 2008.

Garrett, Allison, 'Nose In, Fingers In: The (New?) Role of Corporate Directors', http://internationalcorpgov.blogspot.com/2006/10/nose-in-fingers-in-new-role-of.html, accessed on 9 October 2006.

Gatz, Scott, 'Trusting a Community to Get it Right', retrieved from http://www.scottgatz.com/2006/02/09/trusting-a-community-to-get-it-right/, 9 February 2006.

Gemmill, G., and J. Oakley, 'Leadership: An Alienating Social Myth?' *Human Relations*, Vol. 45, No. 2, 1992, pp. 113–129.

George, Gerard, Randall Sleeth, and Mark Siders, 'Organizing Culture: Leader Roles, Behaviors, And Reinforcement Mechanisms', *Journal Of Business And Psychology*, Vol. 13, No. 4, Summer 1999, pp. 545–60.

Gerstner, L., *Who Says Elephants Can't Dance?*, New York: HarperCollins Inc, 2002.

Greene, Robert, *The 48 Laws of Power*, New York: Penguin Books, 2000.

Haijtema, Dominique, 'The Boss Who Breaks All The Rules', Odemagazine.com, accessed on 19 June 2007.

Harrison, Laird, 'We're All The Boss,' *Time*, Inside Business edition, 8 April 2002.

Harvardbusinessonline.hbsp.harvard.edu

Haslam, Alexander, Stephen Reicher, and Michael Platow, *The New Psychology of Leadership, Identity, Influence and Power*, London: Psychology Press, 2010.

Heifetz, R. A., *Leadership Without Easy Answers*, Cambridge, Massachusetts: Harvard University Press, 1998.

Herbert, Auberon, *The Right and Wrong of Compulsion by the State and Other Essays*, Indianapolis: Liberty Fund, 1978.

Hesselbein, Frances, Marshall Goldsmith (eds.), *The Leader of the Future: New Visions, Strategies, and Practices for the Next Era*, San Francisco: Jossey-Bass, 1996.

Hillis, Laurie, 'Culture Follows The Leader', www.banffcentre.ca/ departments/leadership/.../culture_28–29.pdf, accessed on 19 September 2009.

Hscanada.com

Hunt, Tristam, 'The New Statesman Profile—Robert Putnam', *New Statesman*, 12 March 2001.

Huysman, Marleen, and Volker Wulf (eds), *Social Capital and Information Technology*, Cambridge, Massachusetts: MIT Press, 2004.

Infed.org

Ingo, Henrik, 'Open Life: The Philosophy of Open Source', Translation: Sara Torvalds and edited by Helen Wire, http://openlife.cc, accessed in 2006.

Inquirer.net, 'Business tips from Asia's "Mr. No Frills"', Inquirer.net, accessed on 20 September 2009.

Joe.org

Johansson, Frans, 'Create the Medici Effect', http://hbswk.hbs.edu/archive/4376.html, accessed on 20 September 2004.

Johansson, Frans, *The Medici Effect: Breakthrough Insights at the Intersection of Ideas, Concepts and Cultures*, Cambridge, Massachusetts: Harvard Business School Press, 2004.

Johnson, Craig, *Meeting the Ethical Challenges of Leadership: Casting Light or Shadow*, California: Sage, 2001.

Johnsoncontrols.com

Joi.ito.com

Jouvenel, Bertrand de, *On Power: The Natural History of Its Growth*, Indianapolis: Liberty Press, 1945.

Kanasawa, Santoshi, and Alan Miller, *Why Beautiful People Have More Daughters*, New York: Perigee Trade, 2007.

Kaneshige, Tom, 'Open Source: What You Should Learn From the French', http://www.computerworld.com/s/article/9114165/Open_source_What_you_should_learn_from_the_French?source=rss_topic63, accessed on 28 August 2008.

Kant, Kamal, 'Mentoring for Productivity', http://www.citehr.com/323-mentoring-productivity-kamal-kant.html, accessed on 13 October 2007.

Kiefer, Peter, 'Mafia crime is 7% of GDP in Italy, Group Reports', *The New York Times*, 22 October 2007.

Kiger, Patrick, 'Hidden Hierarchies', *Workforce Management*, 27 February 2006, p. 24.

_____. 'Power of the Individual', *Workforce Management*, 27 February 2006, p. 15.

_____. 'Small Groups, Big Ideas', *Workforce Management*, 27 February 2006, p. 1.

Kilvington, Margaret, Garth Harmsworth, 'The Role of Social Capital in Collaborative Learning', *Landcare Research*, Manaaki Whenua, December 2001.

Kishore, Mohit, 'Tackling Free Riding and Social Loafing', *The Hindu Business Line*, 30 October 2006.

knowledge.wharton.upenn.edu

Knowledge@Emory, 13 September 2001.

Knowledge@Wharton, 'Your Team Too Big? Too Small? What's the Right Number?', 14 June 2006.

Kofman, F. and Peter Senge, 'Communities of Commitment: The Heart of Learning Organizations'. *Organizational Dynamics*, Vol. 22, No. 2, 1993, pp. 5–23.

Kzoo.edu

Lantz, Gayle, 'Business Coaching Can Increase Productivity', http://dallas.bizjurnal.com/dallas/stories/2004/07/26/focus4.html, accessed on 19 February 2009.

Lebow, Rob, and Randy Spitzer, *Accountability—Freedom and Responsibility Without Control*, San Francisco: Berrett-Koehler Publishers, 2002.

Lee, Timothy, 'The Trouble with "Free Riding"', http://www.freedom-to-tinker.com/blog/tblee/trouble-free-riding, accessed on 24 October 2008.

Library.Adelaide.edu.au

Lieberson, S., and J.F. O'Connor, 'Leadership and Organizational Performance: A Study of Large Corporations', *American Sociological Review*, 1972, pp. 117–130.

Lim, Paul J., 'No Ideas? You're Not Alone—If You're in a Group, You'll Have a Better Shot at Being Creative', *U.S. News & World Report*, 10 June 2007.

Linfo.org

List, Christian, Christian Elsholtz, and Thomas Seeley, 'Independence and Interdependence in collective Decision Making: An Agent-Based

Model of Nest-Site Choice by Honey Bee Swarms, personal.lsc.ac.uk/list/pdf-files/honeybees.pdf, accessed on 3 October 2008.

Louisproyect.wordpress.com

MacNeil, Angus, and Alena McClanahan, 'Shared Leadership', *Connexions*, 24 July 2005

Malone, Thomas, *The Future of Work*, Cambridge, Massachusetts: Harvard Business School Press, 2004.

Maresco, Peter A., and Christopher York, *Ricardo Semler: Creating Organizational Change Through Employee Empowered Leadership*, Fairfield, Connecticut: Sacred Heart University, 2005.

Masnick, Michael, 'Free is Not Socialism', http://www.techdirt.com/articles/20081121/0323212915.shtml, accessed on 26 November 2008.

McGuire, Martin C., and Mancur Olson, 'The Economics of Autocracy and Majority Rule: The Invisible Hand and the Use of Force,' *Journal of Economic Literature*, Vol. 34, March 1996, pp. 72–96.

Meindl, J.R., and S.B. Ehrlich, 'The Romance of Leadership and the Evaluation of Organizational Performance', *The Academy of Management Journal*, Vol. 30, No. 1, March 1987, pp. 91–109.

Meindl, J.R., S.B. Ehrlich, and Janet M. Dukerich, 'The Romance of Leadership', *Administrative Science Quarterly*, Vol. 30, No. 1, March 1985, pp. 78–102.

Mendhro, Umaimah, 'A New MBA's View: The Sorry World We're Entering', Forbes.com, accessed on 18 June 2009.

Messina, Chris, 'The Future of Open Leadership', http://factoryjoe.com/blog/2006/06/15/the-future-of-open-leadership/, accessed on 15 June 2009.

Michael, J. A. (Ed.), *For the Common Good: A Strategic Plan for Leadership and Volunteer Development*, Washington DC: United States Department of Agriculture, 1994.

Michele, Erina Doyle, and Mark Smith, 'Classical Leadership', Encyclopedia of Informal Education, http://www.infed.org/leadership/traditional_leadership.htm, accessed in 2001.

Miller, G.J., *Managerial Dilemmas: The Political Economy of Hierarchy*, Cambridge: Cambridge University Press, 1992.

Mintz, Steven, 'The Modern Family', http://www.digitalhistory.uh.edu/historyonline/modernfamily.cfm, accessed on 3 October 2009.

Morgan, Lewis Henry, *Ancient Society: or Researches in the Lines of Human Progress from Savagery through Barbarism to Civilization*, New York: Elibron Classic Series, 2005.

Moss, Stephen, 'Idleness is Good', *The Guardian*, 17 April 2003.

Most, Arnold, 'Creating Empowerment Teams Helps Multiply Productivity', *Plant Engineering*, 1 October 2006, p. 34.

Naidoo, Kumi, 'Lunchtime Address', delivered at World Alliance for Citizen Participation, Secretary General and CEO of CIVICUS, 3 April 2003.

Narayan, Deepa, 'Measuring Empowerment: Cross-Disciplinary Perspectives', Washington, Oxford University Press, September 2006.

Nelson, Barbara, Linda Kaboolian, and Kathryn Carver, *The Concord Handbook: How to Build Social Capital Across Communities*, UCLA School of Public Policy and Social Research, 2003.

Nelson, Nici, and Susan Wright, *Power and Participatory Development: Theory and Practice*, ITDG Publishing, 1995.

Nirenberg, J., *The Living Organization: Transforming Teams into Workplace Communities*, Illinois: Business One Irwin, 1993.

Nye Jr, Joseph, 'Soft Power and Leadership', *Compass: A Journal of Leadership*, Spring 2004.

Okoli, Chitu, and Oh Wonseok, 'Investigating Recognition-Based Performance in an Open Content Community: A Social Capital Perspective', *Information & Management*, Vol. 44, No. 3, April 2007, pp. 240–52.

Olson, Mancur, 'Dictatorship, Democracy, and Development', *American Political Science Review*, Vol. 87, 1993, pp. 567–76.

———. *Power and Prosperity*, New York: Basic Books, November 2000.

Openeverything.wik.is

Openlife.cc

Openlogic.com

Opensource.mit.edu, opensource.mit.edu/papers/hippelkrogh.pdf, accessed on 24 February 2009

Orgdtc.com

Ostrom, E., *Governing the Commons*, Cambridge, UK: Cambridge University Press, 1990.

Owen, Harrison, 'Opening Space For Emerging Order', http://www.openspaceworld.com/brief_history.htm, accessed on 13 October 2009. P2pfoundation.net

Pachauri, R.K., 'Now That's Cricket, Coach', *Indian Express*, 17 September 2006.

Parajuli, Jitendra, 'Social Capital and Open Source Software Movement', campusentrepreneurship.wordpress.com, accessed on 24 September 2008.

Parthasarathy, Vijay, 'Viewpoint: The Role of the Coach in International Sport', *Sports Star*, Vol. 28, No.23, 4–10 June 2005, pp. 4–10. Paulgraham.com

Pearce, Craig, and Jay Conger (eds), *Shared Leadership: Reframing the Hows and Whys*, California: Sage, 2002.

Pearce, Craig L., and C.C. Manz, 'Self and Shared Leadership', *Executive Excellence*, Vol. 21, No. 7, 2007, p. 6.

Pettit, Janis, 'Coaching as a Leadership Tool to Increase Productivity', carolinanewswire.com, accessed on 22 November 2004.

Phillips, Katherine, 'Diversity Helps Your Business—But Not The Way You Think', Forbes.com, accessed on 23 July 2009.

Phillips, Katherine, and Katie Liljenquist, 'The Advantages and Liabilities of Agreeing With Socially Distinct Newcomers', *Personality and Social Psychology Bulletin*, March 2009, pp. 336–50.

Pickering, Chris, 'IT's Tragedy of the Commons', itmanagement.earthweb.com, accessed on 8 April 2002.

Platt, John, 'Social Traps', *American Psychologist*, August 1973, pp. 641–51.

Pradhan, Kunal, 'Roles and Regulations, But Who's the Boss?', Indianexpress.com, 10 January 2009.

Pritchard, Chris, 'Asia's Answer to Richard Branson', *The Sydney Morning Herald*, 22 August 2008.

Putnam, Robert D., 'Institutional Performance and Political Culture in Italy: Some Puzzles about the Power of the Past', Harvard University Center for European Studies, Working Paper Series, 1987.

Putnam, Robert, Robert Leonardi, *Making Democracy Work: Civic Traditions in Modern Italy*, Princeton: Princeton University Press, 1993.

Putnam, Robert, *Bowling Alone: The Collapse and Revival of American Community*, New York: Simon and Schuster, 2000.

Putnam, Robert, (ed.) *Democracies in Flux: The Evolution of Social Capital in Contemporary Society*, New York: Oxford University Press, 2002.

Puzo, Mario, *The Godfather*, adapted screenplay for the movie, 1972.

Rahman, Khondaker Mirazur, 'Ray of Light: Dav Whatmore, Savior of Bangladesh Cricket', www.banglacricket.com, accessed on 13 March 2007.

Ramsey, Robert D., *Don't Teach the Canaries Not to Sing: Creating a School Culture that Boosts Achievement*, California: Sage, 2007.

Raymond, Eric S., 'The Cathedral and the Bazaar', *O'Reilly Media*, October 1999.

Resnick, Mitchel, 'Beyond the Centralized Mindset', *Journal of the Learning Sciences*, Vol. 5, No. 1, 1996, pp. 1–22.

Results.org

Ridpath, Mike, 'How to Create a Corporate Culture that Inspires its Workforce', Hooverwebdesign.com, accessed on 10 October 2009.

Riehle.org

Rosen, Keith, 'A Question On Full Accountability–What's The Reward for Management and Executives?', *All Business*, 26 November 2008, p. 45.

Rosen, Keith, 'Embrace Full Accountability–For Everything and Everyone', http://www.allbusiness.com/company-activities-management/sales-selling/11675109-1.htm, accessed on 18 November 2008.

Sandmann, Lorilee R., and Lela Vandenberg, 'A Framework for 21st Century Leadership', *Journal of Extension*, Vol. 33, December 1995.

Santos, Boaventura de Sousa, 'Participatory Budgeting in Porto Alegre: Toward a Redistributive Democracy', *Politics & Society*, December 1998, pp. 461–510.

Saxon, Miki, 'Start as a Nut, End as a Leader', http://www.leadershipturn.com/start-as-a-nut-end-as-a-leader/, accessed on 21 September 2007.

Schein, E., 'Notes from Cape Cod Seminar', August 2002.

Schindler, Esther, 'Leadership Lessons: Passion, Smarts and What Open Source Can Learn About Management', http://advice.cio.com/ esther–schindler/leadership–lessons, accessed on 22 July 2008.

Selfhelp.on.ca

Selfhelpgroups.org

Semler, Ricardo, *Maverick*, New York: Grand Central Publishing, 1995.

Semler, Ricardo, 'How We Went Digital Without a Strategy', *Harvard Business Review*, Vol. 78, September 2000, pp. 3–8.

Semler, Ricardo, 'Seven-Day Weekend', *Portfolio*, March 2004.

Semler, Ricardo, 'Why My Former Employees Still Work for Me', *Harvard Business Review*, March 2009

Shambaugh, Rebecca, 'Glass Ceiling or Sticky Floor? The Real Reason Women Don't Make it', *Washington Business Journal*, 3 March 2006.

Shermer, Michael, *Why People Believe Weird Things*, New York: W.H. Freeman, 1997.

Shutterasia.com

Siisiäinen, Martti, 'Two Concepts of Social Capital: Bourdieu vs Putnam', paper presented at ISTR Fourth International Conference, Trinity College, Dublin, Ireland 5–8 July 2000.

Singh, Param Vir, Yong Tan, and Vijay Mookerjee, 'Network Effects: The Influence of Structural Social Capital on Open Source Project Success', Research paper, April 2008.

Sirianni, Carmen, and Lewis Friedland, 'Social Capital', *Civic Practices Network*, 2001.

Skyscrapercity.com

Slater, Philip, 'America's Love Affair with the Mafia', http://www. huffingtonpost.com/philip-slater/americas-love-affair-wit_b_45579. html, accessed on 11 April 2007.

Smith, Peter, *Team Technologies*, Section 8, Leadership, Maine: Cumberland, 1995.

Spitzer, Randal, 'What Really Motivates People', http://searchwarp.com/ swa74908.htm, accessed on 27 June 2006.

Spolsky, Joel, 'How Hard Could It Be? My Style of Servant Leadership', http://www.inc.com/magazine/20081201/how-hard-could-it-be-my-style-of-servant-leadership.html, accessed on 1 December 2008.

Stallard, Michael Lee, 'It's All About Team Work', *Economic Times*, Corporate Dossier, 22 August 2008.

Stein, Howard F., 'Organizational Totalitarianism And The Voices Of Dissent', jop.missouri.edu/Organizational Totalitarianism.pdf, accessed on 9 June 2009.

Sullivan, John, 'Hidden Passion', http://www.workforce.com/archive/feature/25/76/50, accessed on 8 October 2009.

Swvolunteerinitiative.org.au

Taylor, William, 'The Leader of the Future', http://www.fastcompany.com/magazine/25/heifetz.html, accessed on 19 December 2007.

Thomas, Nancy, and Scott Saslow, 'Improving Productivity through Coaching and Mentoring', http://www.mentorresources.com/CLO_Improving_Productivity.doc, accessed on 5 October 2009.

Trimmer, Anne, 'Accountability: Lessons learnt from the private sector', http://www.allbusiness.com/management-companies-enterprises/297999-1.html, accessed on 1 May 2009.

Tucker, Ross, 'Gore's Kelly: No Titles, All Team', *Women's Wear Daily*, 16 November 2005, p. 34.

Usher, Rod, 'Heat on the Mob', http://www.time.com/time/international/1996/960603/mafia.html, accessed on 3 June 2010.

Varese, Federico, 'How Mafias Migrate: The Case of the 'Ndrangheta in Northern Italy', *Law and Society Review*, Vol. 40, No. 2, 2006, pp. 411–444.

Varghese, Sangeeth, 'Decide to Lead', *Business World*, 2009.

Viswanath, G., 'A Cricket Coach is the Support Base for the Captain', *Sports Star*, Vol. 24, No. 44, 3–9 November 2001, pp. 3–9.

Waghorn, Terry, 'How One Company Makes Its Employees All Visionaries', Forbes.com, accessed on 30 June 2009.

Wagner, Tony, 'The Buddy System', Teachermagazine.com, accessed on 1 January 2005.

Warr, Deborah J., 'Social networks in a "Discredited" Neighborhood', *Journal of Sociology*, 1 September 2005, pp. 285–308.

Watson, Julia, 'Opening Up Leadership at Open Everything', http://communicopia.com/blog/opening-leadership-open-everything, accessed on 24 September 2008.

Wearethebest.wordpress.com

Web.worldbank.org

Weber, Steve, *The Success of Open Source*, Cambridge, Massachusetts, Harvard University Press, 2004.

Weinreb, Michael, 'Power to the People', *Sales & Marketing Management*, April 2003.

Wieners, Brad, 'Ricardo Semler: Set Them Free', http://www.cioinsight. com/c/a/Expert-Voices/Ricardo-Semler-Set-Them-Free/, accessed in April 2009.

Wikinomics.com

Wikipedia.com

Wilkins, Rachel, 'The One Cleveland Effect: New Models of Open Source Leadership', http://blog.case.edu/lev.gonick/2005/10/16/ the_onecleveland_effect_new_models_of_open_source_leadership, accessed on 28 October 2005.

Windley, Phil, 'Paul Graham on Open Source and Blogging', http:// blogs.zdnet.com/BTL/index.php?p=1669&tag=nl.e539, accessed on 2 August 2005.

Winston, Bruce E., 'Toward a New Understanding of Leader Accountability: Defining a Critical Construct', *Journal of Leadership & Organizational Studies*, 1 January 2005, pp. 84–94.

Wired.com

Woolcock, Michael and Deepa Narayan, 'Social Capital: Implications for Development Theory, Research, and Policy', *World Bank Research Observer*, 2000, pp. 225–249.

Workforce Management, '1995 Optimas Awards', 1995.

Yeates, Stuart, 'Open Source Leadership: Debian', http://www.oss-watch. ac.uk/resources/debianleader.xml, accessed in September 2006.

Yunwen, Ye, and Kishida Kouichi, 'Toward an Understanding of the Motivation of Open Source Software Developers', icse, p. 419, 25th International Conference on Software Engineering, 2003.

Zeromillion.com

Index